T0348399

Managing banking relationships

The Association of Corporate Treasurers

The Association of Corporate Treasurers is a professional body, formed in May 1979, to encourage and promote the study and practice of finance and treasury management, and to educate and train those involved in this field. The Association currently has 1800 Members, 600 Associates and more than 1500 students. It is the only UK body which concentrates and sets professional examinations exclusively on the subject of finance and treasury management. The Association is an independent body, governed by a Council of Members whose work is supported by a number of active voluntary committees.

Managing banking relationships

Edited by
Gerald Leahy

WOODHEAD PUBLISHING LIMITED

with

THE ASSOCIATION OF
CORPORATE TREASURERS

Published by Woodhead Publishing Limited with The Association of Corporate Treasurers

Woodhead Publishing Limited,
80 High Street, Sawston, Cambridge CB22 3HJ, UK
www.woodheadpublishing.com; www.woodheadpublishingonline.com

Woodhead Publishing, 1518 Walnut Street, Suite 1100, Philadelphia, PA 19102-3406, USA

Woodhead Publishing India Private Limited, G-2, Vardaan House,
7/28 Ansari Road, Daryaganj, New Delhi – 110002, India
www.woodheadpublishingindia.com

First published 1997, Woodhead Publishing Limited
© Woodhead Publishing Limited and The Association of Corporate Treasurers, 1997
The authors have asserted their moral rights.

British Library Cataloguing in Publication Data
A catalogue record for this book is available from the British Library.

ISBN 978-1-85573-326-8

Contents

Foreword

A measure of any financial system is the ease and flexibility with which investors are linked to those who are in need of capital funds. A key part of this process is the relationship between borrower and lender. Like all successful relationships, it needs to create shared benefits, and be based on mutual understanding.

It is certainly true that the rapid development of financial markets and product innovation in the 1980s and 1990s has changed the nature of banking relationships, not least because it has increased the number of methods for raising corporate finance and consequently the number of players in the market. As part of this change, some products and markets have become highly transactions based, and thus little by way of a relationship exists between the parties on either side. Whilst there are good economic and commercial reasons for such developments, the establishment of a banking relationship in other areas of corporate finance is just as important as it ever was, and this is true both in the good times and the bad.

The establishment of a relationship is not easy; indeed it is in the nature of the banking relationship that there are difficulties to overcome. Most important, there is the flow of information which has to take place so that the bank can initially assess, and subsequently monitor, the borrower effectively. Failing to ensure an effective flow of information typically results in the lender charging a higher margin to compensate for the lack of information, or, in extremis, a refusal to lend. But, by establishing sound relationships, and managing them efficiently, such problems can be overcome.

From our own involvement with the 'London Approach', which has evolved since the late 1970s to assist in situations where, typically, a company in difficulty needs to seek financial support and has to agree this with the many banks with which it has lending relationships, we have seen the value of good relationships between borrower and lender. But, macroeconomic policy has a vital part to play here too. The authorities must ensure that the backdrop to lending decisions, and maintaining sound banking relationships, is an economy which does not suffer from the boom-bust cycles that we have seen all too often in the past. This requires a firm commitment to stability-orientated policies, and I am encouraged that in many countries around the world, including the UK, clear progress can be seen towards achieving this kind of stable environment.

Within such an environment, borrowers and lenders can concentrate on the important work that they must do to build solid relationships. For lenders this means having a clear understanding of the borrower's business, which is essential to ensure a flow of lending which is tailored to the particular needs of the borrower. For the borrower this means having a clear understanding of the objectives of, and the constraints on, the lender and the information it requires. Only with all of this framework in place, macroeconomic and microeconomic, can we create an atmosphere of understanding and trust, in which a long term relationship can prosper.

By helping to promote better understanding between borrower and lender, I have no doubt that this book will make an important contribution to corporate finance.

Eddie George
Governor
Bank of England

Editor's introduction

This book has been some time in the making. This is not the fault of the authors who have shown great patience in responding to the requests of their editor to review and update their chapters as new material required inclusion. As one asked plaintively – 'Did *War and Peace* take this long?'

So far the 1990s have been years of upheaval in the banking industry and turmoil in industry, thanks to recession, restructuring and changes in regulation. At the end of the 1980s, many in banking talked of banking relationships as things of the past. Yet in 1997 banking relationships are in robust health with both sides knowing what they want from the relationship. This book sets out to explain why and how.

Every author is an expert in his own field and very senior in his organisation. That they have given so freely and patiently of their time is testimony to the importance they attribute to this subject. Between them, they have decades of experience. A constant theme throughout is that trust, integrity and the ability to see the other's point of view are the key to good banking relationships – that is, profitable to both sides.

In exercising the editorial role, I have tried to adopt a light touch by allowing the inevitable differences in style to come through, whilst eliminating unnecessary overlap and adopting common terminology. There is still some overlap but covering the same theme from two divergent views can be helpful.

The first four chapters are intended to be introductory covering the developments in banking over the last decade; the services available from commercial and investment banking and how they impact relationships; and a broad overview of the current regulatory climate.

The next two chapters deal with policy matters giving insights into why corporates and banks act in the way they do. There follow two chapters, one from each side on practical aspects of setting up a relationship.

Chapter 9 consists of three case studies; two of which deal with difficult aspects of banking relationships; the third can be seen as a model of how to set up and run rewarding relationships. All three are corporate as banks are precluded from revealing such information because of confidentiality rules.

Chapter 10 deals with the inevitability of relationships coming to an end but the need for this to be done with finesse whichever side takes the initiative.

Finally there is an attempt to look ahead to see what continuous banking changes might do to relationships and for which I have to the responsibility myself.

List of contributors

This book is based on contributions from the following:

Chapters 1 and 5, John Grout – Finance Director of the Confectionery Stream at Cadbury Schweppes plc. Prior to his current role, John was Director of Treasury for Cadbury Schweppes plc.

Chapter 2, R V Emerson – Group Head, Corporate Banking, Standard Chartered Bank, Singapore until 1996. He was previously Director and General Manager, Banking at Nomura Bank International.

Chapter 3, Kleinwort Benson.

Chapter 4, A J Herbert – head of Allen & Overy's corporate department, specialising in international offerings, equity and debt and became a partner in 1970. The author was aided in the preparation of this chapter by Judith Cseh-Menczer.

Chapter 6, J A Donaldson – retired from the position of Group Treasurer of Imperial Chemical Industries plc in 1986 and is currently a director of The MTM Partnership Limited.

Chapter 7, T H Donaldson – from 1974 until his retirement in 1996, Thomas Donaldson was Morgan Guaranty's senior, and for a long time only, credit specialist, first in London and then in Europe.

Chapter 8, A R Prindl – joined Nomura International Ltd as Managing Director in 1984. He is now Chairman of Nomura Bank International plc, which he founded. NBI opened in 1986 and is the hub of banking services for the Nomura Group.

Chapter 9, Judith Harris-Jones – a Partner at Arthur Andersen; Brad Asher – a freelance journalist; Michael MacCallan – Group Treasurer of the Cookson Group plc.

Chapter 10, Robert K Ankrom – formerly Managing Director of RJR Industries.

Chapter 11, Gerald Leahy.

1 On banks

No one has ever actually liked bankers, it seems. The aristocracy despised them because they were in trade. The poor despised them because they were rich. Borrowers and would-be borrowers, whatever their station, feared them (generally) because they were powerful and (specifically) because they owed them money; and bankers were disliked because they either would not lend, or, having lent, wanted their money back – with interest. Even today some bank customers appear to find it strange that banks should want their money back and with interest.

Banks defined

What, then, is a bank?

> In 1972, representatives of a major UK bank asked the Bank of England how a bank was defined in the United Kingdom. The Principal of the Bills Office replied 'In this country, a bank is a bank if I regard it as a bank (Gottfried O Bruder, 26 October 1993, to a dinner of the CBI London Region).

Precise legal definitions are hard to come by. *Hasbury's Laws of England* (4th edition) declines to define a bank but does define 'banking': 'the receipt of money on current or deposit account and the payment of cheques drawn by and the collection of cheques paid in by a customer'. *The Oxford English Dictionary* is much more helpful, defining a bank as an establishment for taking deposits and making money by lending them out. It also reminds us of the word's origins. Originally a shelf, later a bench, 'bank' was extended to mean a counter or money-changer's table. The concept of banking developed in the Middle Ages. When a merchant brought his coin for safe-keeping to someone trustworthy who had a strong-box – in England commonly a quaker or a goldsmith – it was credited to this account. A note to the goldsmith enabled the merchant to pay out some of the deposit to another or even to transfer some of it to the account of another merchant. This permitted payment without the dangers of moving the actual coin through the streets. It also avoided the risk of being paid in false or 'clipped' coin.

The breakthrough came when it was realised that the coin deposited for safe-keeping could be lent, not merely stored. The lending earned interest for the deposit taker then, not for the depositor. Indeed, if the borrower was going to use the loan to pay another customer of the deposit taker, actual coin did not need to be lent at all. So the deposit taker could lend out more than the deposits he had taken. It was sufficient for the borrower to be told that his account had been credited with the sum and that the deposit taker would accept instructions to transfer that sum to others. This realisation created banking in its modern sense. For it to work properly, the original depositors and the borrowers or the holders of notes they have issued must not all come for their coin at the same time. They must continue to trust the bank. For the magic to work, the bank must be sufficiently profitable and have sufficient capital for confidence to be maintained.

Accordingly, though they may doubt it when paying interest and bank charges, it is of key importance to clients that their banks are profitable. How much profit a bank makes will depend on a variety of factors not least of which is the current balance of power between the bank and its customers – the main theme of this book.

With these origins it is not surprising that banks today are relied on by companies (and others) for deposit taking and lending and various kinds of money transmission and exchange services. In addition, trading in or underwriting of securities and negotiable instruments and financial futures and options, commodities trading, managing investments, acting as custodians or depositories, issuing guarantees and (in some jurisdictions, or) letters of credit, giving advice and selling insurance (and many other things too) are all undertaken by various banks. Moreover, today, many non-banks compete with banks in providing all these services; about the only area where banks have the field more or less to themselves is the provision of undrawn credit, i.e. stand-by lines. The institutions allowed to call themselves banks and the business they are allowed to undertake vary according to the history of the jurisdiction within which they operate.

The term 'bank' has, then, been used more or less loosely around the world and at different times. In this book the word will be used to refer to a wide variety of financial institutions, whatever they are called in any particular place. When used without qualification, we will normally mean by 'bank' an institution that accepts deposits of money (which become its liabilities) and generally invests those deposits by making loans (which become its assets). The bank's income is generally expected to arise from charging borrowers more in interest than is lost in payment of interest to depositors and in lending to borrowers who neglect to repay.

Banks classified

In discussing banks it is usual to draw up convenient classifications. Increasingly the lines of differentiation are becoming blurred as the banking industry is going through a major bout of mergers, takeovers and restructuring, so some caution is needed in looking at convenient classifications.

Commercial banks

These, if not state-owned, are usually large companies quoted on the stock exchanges of their home country (and possibly others). Commercial banks usually have large branch networks which historically have enabled them to gather deposits from the general public. They have capital bases (hence the need for stock exchange listing) to support the deposit taking and lending. Through the branches they lend to the public and small and medium-sized enterprises and provide money transmission services, foreign exchange, and investment advice. Through regional or head offices they lend to large enterprises and take deposits from them too.

In most countries there are perhaps four to ten main domestic commercial banks. In the UK there are currently six, often called *the clearers* or 'the clearing banks', so-called because of their dominance of the central cheque clearing system for English and Scottish banks. Today's system is open to more banks, but, in the past, membership was a decisive advantage in the sterling banking market.

The US has many thousand commercial banks due to a proliferation of state-level banking laws. Even here, however, commercial banking is dominated by fewer than 15 *money-centre* (New York) and *super-regional* banks. Some big banks do not have large branch networks and are dependent on taking large deposits from corporations and borrowing from other banks and institutions to fund their lending. These banks are sometimes called *wholesale banks* as opposed to the *retail banks* with their large branch networks.

A key feature of commercial banks which does not necessarily apply to other 'banks' is their relationship to a *central bank*. The central bank provides them with a 'lender of last resort'. This means that an illiquid but otherwise solvent bank which is subject to demands for payment that it otherwise would be unable to meet will be lent unlimited funds by the central bank. A spectacular modern example of this was brought about by a computer failure at the Bank of New York in November 1985. This prevented the bank completing certain operations. It necessitated the bank's going to the 'Discount Window' of the US Federal Reserve System (the US central bank) to borrow $US22.6 billion in addition to an overdraft of $1 billion, to meet its obligations on the day. The price of this privileged status with the central bank is that the central bank regulates and supervises the commercial banks and, usually, the deposit taking activity of other banks.

French commercial banks are very similar to UK clearing banks. The three major French banks also have a significant and long standing presence in the UK. They have also developed partnership arrangements with German banks especially to address opportunities in Eastern Europe.

German commercial banking is somewhat different in that it embraces a wide range of activities including investment banking (see below). The term 'universal' bank is often used to describe the biggest banks indicating the 'universality' of their range of activities. This term is also used widely in Switzerland and the Netherlands.

Japanese commercial banks divide into city and regional and are again slightly different, engaging in some investment banking activities but not others from which they are excluded.

These slight variations between countries reflect the historical development and regulatory independence in each jurisdiction. To repeat the note of caution in the beginning of this chapter, however, the banking scene is changing so quickly that it is likely that in a relatively short period it will be almost impossible to discern real differences between the largest banks anywhere.

Investment banks

The term 'investment bank' has a US heritage but has been increasingly adopted throughout the world. In the US it indicates not only a provider of long term funds to industry, both debt and equity, but also an underwriter and dealer in securities and a provider of corporate finance advice. Investment banks in the US, then, combine the role of British merchant banks (see below), stockbrokers (US brokers are called price takers) and market makers (US dealers are called price makers). This pattern of investment banking is increasingly being adopted worldwide.

In the UK, merchant banks, which as their name implies originally specialised in trade-related activities, had long since become synonymous with corporate finance activities (see Chapter 3), raising debt and equity and advising on mergers and acquisitions. This did not require large amounts of capital but did call for highly talented and creative people. The breakdown of barriers to the free flow of capital, global competition and the development of investment banking with its ability to commit large amounts of own capital, combined to force the merchant banks to reassess their strategy. Those that decided they had to be bigger and – following the UK Stock Exchange reforms of 1986 – had to have market making capability, set out to turn themselves into investment banks (while still retaining the old name of merchant banks). In the event, the leading players failed in the enterprise. It was insufficient capital and a loss of direction that drove Morgan Grenfell into the arms of Deutsche Bank in 1989 followed in 1995 by perhaps the most illustrious name in merchant banking, namely SG Warburg, being acquired by Swiss Bank Corporation. This event was the most dramatic evidence of the decline of the merchant banks as independent houses. Yet if the example of Morgan Grenfell is to be followed it does not mean the end of these activities in London; quite the reverse, since Deutsche Bank is building its global investment banking through Deutsche Morgan Grenfell in London and SBC looks set to do the same with SBC Warburg. Other Continental European banks are building their investment banking businesses in London from scratch. An example is Westdeutsche LandesBank which is developing West Merchant Bank.

Perhaps the saddest manifestation of the changes in 1994/1995 was the collapse of Barings in February 1995, due as much as anything to the inability of its management to understand and control derivatives trading. Barings was snapped up by the Dutch group ING which only came together in 1991 by a merger between the big insurance company Nationale Nederlanden and NMB PostBank.

Despite some of the biggest names – Kleinwort Benson was bought by Dresdner Bank in 1995 – becoming part of big international banks, other famous names have retained their independence, such as Schroders, Lazard, Rothschild and Flemings.

Other banks

Savings banks (mainly on the mainland of Europe and as state-licensed institutions in the US), building societies (in the UK), savings and loan associations (US), credit unions (US) and other bodies have developed which focus on the retail (personal) client and are not considered further. They are often regulated not by the central bank but by a special body. Some have become more like commercial banks, however, or have formally changed into them (e.g. Abbey National Plc).

Most co-operative banks specialise in personal business, but there are others specialising in lending to particular industries, some of which, like France's Crédit Agricole, have begun to widen their horizons.

Finally, there are internationally and nationally sponsored investment banks such as the World Bank, the Inter-American Development Bank and the European Investment Bank. These behave more or less like commercial banks in their permitted range of activities but may be able to provide types of funding (especially as regards maturity or price) not commercially available.

Are banks 'special'?

In many countries banks, particularly commercial banks, are seen to be special, usually privileged, members of the financial community. Commercial banks benefit from a 'lender of last resort' and from regulatory barriers to entry to the industry. In some countries they benefit from being able to offer government or government-backed guarantees to depositors. Why is this?

The attitude of the regulators of commercial banks is well articulated by the US Federal Reserve. Banks are special because of their key roles in the payments system (which depends on confidence), in the credit granting process, and in conveying monetary policy to other economic players.

Others take the view that the protection and restrictions that the authorities' view of the 'specialness' of commercial banks induces are simply ways of protecting inefficient banks. For example, the US insistence that other financial or industrial corporations should not own banks, regardless of whether they have sufficient capital and adequate management, prevents the takeover of poorly run banks.

An insight into the Bank of England's view of this is given by the evidence given to the inspectors undertaking in 1992 the second inquiry into the role of National Westminster Bank in the 1987 Blue Arrow rights issue. Brian Quinn, Bank director in charge of supervision, is quoted thus:

> We have ... a preference for avoiding official investigations into banks. Banks are essentially about confidence, and the mere knowledge that there might be an investigation conducted on an official basis into a bank can have an effect on confidence that we think is damaging.

As the economic and business environment fluctuates, so the regulations are varied to permit or prevent new entries to banking or new owners for banks. While regulators, however, are convinced banks are special, decisions by the US Federal Reserve and most recently by the Bank of England in the case of Barings show that regulators are not prepared to save banks from their own folly. The key factor has been whether in allowing a bank to fail there is any systemic risk which might cause a threat to the banking system.

The development of banks internationally

As companies have expanded overseas they have looked to familiar banks to service them. In recent decades, however, large banks, finding it difficult to increase an already large market share at home, have looked abroad not just to service existing clients, but for growth. Companies in the host countries have welcomed the incomers too as a force to break down the oligopolies of their handful of indigenous large banks.

First into Europe on a large scale were the large American commercial banks which grew through the 1970s. With few formal capital adequacy constraints they geared up their initially well capitalised balance sheets and were able to lend at lower margins than previously seen. Equally important, they brought in specialists in providing services to companies, operating in teams from their local head offices. Indigenous banks at that time handled even large corporate customers from 'convenient' branches along with retail customers and small firms. The incomers, not surprisingly, were much better placed to sell the more modern services as they developed.

Japanese banks followed into Europe and European banks began to compete more strongly in other European countries during the 1970s and 1980s. But so far none has established the presence of the Americans at their peak.

During the 1980s, the indigenous banks became more aggressive in pricing, reorganised themselves to serve large companies through dedicated teams and set up the specialised departments to provide the products such customers needed.

By the end of that decade, the American commercial banks, hurt by provisions for bad or non-performing loans (first advances to third world sovereign risks, then advances to the property sector and general lending) were cutting back their international networks and no longer pricing advances aggressively. Some European banks (notably, but not only, the British) had problems of their own. With the start of the 1990s, Japanese banks too were constrained, in their case not only by the need to meet new, stricter, capital adequacy requirements but also by potential and actual losses on securities portfolios and in (mainly domestic) lending to troubled sectors.

At any time of constraint, banks have good reasons to give priority to their home markets where they usually have strong positions. Reinforcing or falling back on (relative) success may be the best strategy. However, political considerations also mean priority for the home country.

Accordingly, even in the UK (in many ways the most open of markets) while international banks are a permanent feature, indigenous banks are again a force to be reckoned with.

Banking relationships

The relationships a company can have with a bank range from close to distant, good to bad, wide-ranging to narrowly focused, long lasting to ephemeral. In many ways they are as much personal as institutional: they should normally be relationships of trust and professionalism. The institutions are important, however: a company cannot have the same relationship with Barclays Bank or Deutsche Bank as it has with a small US investment banking boutique.

In simplest presentation, banking relationships are generally polarised into 'transactional' and 'relationship' in character. In this two category model, *transaction relationships* are taken to be those in which a company keeps banks at a distance, gives them limited information and seeks quotations for all its business from many banks. It awards the business to the bank with the lowest price or most favourable terms and conditions, and will move it away swiftly again if a competitor with a better offer is identified.

Relationship banking, at its extreme, is where a company has a very small number of banks – if not one alone – with which it has dealt for many decades. These banks have a detailed knowledge of the company's business, kept up to date by regular briefings. Business is awarded to the banks (or bank) whatever the price and whatever the conditions.

Most corporate client relationships with banks fall between the two extremes, shifting one way or the other over time. Although as John Kay (Chairman, London Economics and director, School of Management Studies at Oxford University) has observed: 'It is easier to move away from relational contracts than towards them.'

The pendulum swings

Until the development of international banking in the 1970s, banking relationships were often personal and of long standing. Some countries still had strict rules governing the flow of capital so there was less incentive for companies to shop around.

The arrival of foreign banks on the domestic market together with the relaxation of restrictions on capital flows brought a new era of competition. Foreign banks, in particular, with no assured base of domestic business, tended to develop 'one-off' pieces of business. They often sent their brightest people abroad so the scene was set for what became known as transaction banking.

The high point of transaction banking was to be seen in the latter part of the 1980s when banks were competing fiercely for business, and many companies found it hard to resist the temptation to take the lowest price. It was also mainly an Anglo-US phenomenon although French companies also entered enthusiastically into transaction banking. Other countries tended to have a more stable banking picture, Germany and Japan in particular.

The recession of 1990–1991 brought an end to the most extreme forms of transaction banking. Many companies began to reassess their relationships, reducing them whenever possible to a 'core' group with which confidential information could be shared. 'Core' group banking, known on the Continent of Europe as 'house' banks, has long been favoured in countries such as Germany, the Netherlands and Switzerland.

It was a time, too, when several large companies on both sides of the Atlantic required rescue. It was then that companies became aware of the disadvantages of having a multitude of banks in a syndicate with little knowledge of the company and even less desire to be part of a rescue operation. There is one well known 'rescue' meeting at which the company did not have a room large enough to accommodate all the banks in the syndicate.

As the bubble burst, margins in favour of banks improved

dramatically but since 1993 the pendulum has once more swung back in favour of companies. The September 1995 survey on 'Corporate Credit Policy in the UK' carried out by ACT and Bank Relationship Consulting shows that in the UK at least, margins are still declining and this trend was confirmed by the Standard & Poor's survey (December 1995).

Nevertheless, a return to 'transaction' banking on the scale seen in the 1980s looks doubtful. Corporate memories are not that short. In any case, companies would argue that margins are under pressure everywhere in today's economic climate. It is doubtful, however, whether there is another industry which sees such rapid swings in the balance of power between provider and customer.

The importance of capital adequacy

The recession of 1990–1991 tended to disguise a more fundamental change in banks' attitude to lending. Alarmed by the weakened state of many large bank balance sheets, the Bank for International Settlements (BIS) set out new rules for capital adequacy which the central banks agreed to implement with effect from January 1993. The European Union has further emphasised these in its 'Capital Adequacy Directive'. The aim is to ensure that banks have appropriate levels of capital to support their business. The new rules mean, for example, that banks can lend with zero capital for credit risk to OECD governments but need significant capital for credit risk from the private sector. Intermediate amounts of capital are required for local government lending (see Chapter 4, pp. 45–46).

One effect should be to eliminate unfair competition by one bank adopting a 'loss leader' approach. Another, already evident, is that banks are cutting back on direct lending to the corporate sector. In the US, according to Federal Reserve Bank of San Francisco March 1993 figures, business loans have fallen from one-third of American commercial banks' financial assets in the first half of the 1970s to only one-fifth today. The US banks have filled the gap by buying US government bonds.

Furthermore, because over the long run the principal generator of bank capital is retained earnings, setting minimum capital requirements backing banks' assets also sets a minimum rate of return to the bank in its regulated activities. In general, higher return is associated with higher risk. Accordingly, banks may be driven to seek business in unrelated areas or to restrict business with low risk private sector clients in favour of those who must concede higher reward to the banks.

Pressure on banks' balance sheets can be seen in their drive towards fee-earning services (broking, or perhaps promises to do things in the future rather than actually doing them now) and away from interest-spread-earning lending in their business with clients.

The illiquidity of loans (to individuals and countries as well as corporates) has been a key factor in bank profitability as they intermediate between borrowers and lenders. The difficulty of assessing the credit standing of individual borrowers also gave banks a key role as lenders' 'delegated monitors' of credit worthiness. The increasing importance of credit rating agencies, coupled with the creation of secondary markets – in impaired debt of sovereign borrowers, in bundles of residential mortgages, credit card and other customer loans – have changed the picture, reducing the capital required to originate the loans (before reselling them). Secondary markets in corporate loans, both 'good' and 'impaired', have begun to stir. In some cases secondary markets are securitised and in others the markets are for whole loans or specific participations in them. If loan agreements prevent selling of loans by banks, they may get round this by selling 'silent sub-participations' which pass on the economic but not the legal relationship and need no borrower consent.

All this helps banks' liquidity, capital adequacy and return-on-capital problems and it can be argued that companies may benefit from implied lower costs and that, in cases of impaired loans, institutions specializing in 'difficult situations' may be better able to support companies. It may disrupt any relationship between borrower and lender during the life of the loan; it may mean that a client cannot control which institutions it is actually borrowing from or its relationship with them. How can the borrower, for example, anticipate who will be interpreting, relaxing or reapplying covenants or default conditions? Perhaps companies will press for the introduction of trustees between themselves and lenders as with Eurobonds. In any case, the development denies to both banks and customers 'the flexibility to relationship banking [which] permits bankers to attempt to go that extra yard when bad things happen to good people' (J F Sinkey Jr, *Commercial Bank Financial Management in the Financial Services Industry*, Macmillan, 1991).

2 Relationships in commercial banking

This chapter is concerned with the way different banking services impact the relationship with a client and, indeed, whether the term relationship has any real value in describing activities between companies and their banking 'suppliers' in this highly competitive and fast moving world.

The late 1980s and early 1990s saw a protracted recessionary environment which tested the relationship concept pretty thoroughly, causing companies and banks to rethink the nature of the idea. For many, on both sides, it was a rude awakening. Certainly, over the period banking strategies ebbed and flowed between relationship and product driven, transaction-based approaches to their clients, as banks tried to deal with thinning margins in oversupplied markets. After all, why grace a piece of business with the term relationship if requirements are limited and specific; if it is truly only an arm's length buying and selling process? The need for clarity is critical: what often defines a relationship in the good times is unlikely to sustain it in the bad times, and it is only at that point that many companies discover that they do not have a relationship at all. It is therefore crucial to know at all times, not only the current intentions of each party, but also their likely future appetites. It was a failure to understand this that led to many of the problems that emerged during the recession of the late 1980s and early 1990s. Indeed it is just this issue which highlights a critical difference in the nature of relationships between merchant/investment banks and their clients, and commercial banks and their clients, a point which will be explored later.

In all of this recent change and trauma, one thing has emerged clearly: the ability and willingness to provide finance still lies at the core of all true banking relationships.

Sources of finance

Over the past decade there has been a substantial increase in sources of finance, from equity through an increasingly wide range of debt instruments.

The issues for raising equity are vast compared with, say, borrowing short term money market funds to cover overnight shortfalls in liquidity. Nevertheless, the bank providing this latter service may well feel it is at least part of some relationship; otherwise why would they be doing it, because they are unlikely to be making any money from the service! The equity side, however, does highlight some of the key relationship issues:

(a) Confidence. The issuing company must believe that its adviser knows the market intimately such that the timing and pricing of the issue will ensure its success. Clearly, this cannot be achieved without, in turn, the bank having an intimate knowledge of the company itself, especially the management at board level. This kind of knowledge is not acquired quickly (nor by watching the television news). Personalities, their likes and dislikes, appetites and fears, have to be understood; and herein lies a critical factor – visibility and image. Failure of an issue involves public embarrassment which goes all the way up to the chief executive level, and retribution will come all the way down from there. This will be particularly true if the raising of equity is linked to some major investment or expansion on the part of the company.

(b) Integrity. The information required in this area is highly sensitive for very obvious reasons. The company must have complete trust, not just in the *intentions* of the bank to keep the information secret but, more importantly, its *ability* to do so; are internal controls adequate? Again, this type of trust is not built up quickly or easily.

Whatever the levels of technical expertise a bank may claim, these cannot be sold to a company without there being already a relationship of trust in place, and this can only be established over time and at several different levels in the two organisations, all the way up to the top.

The borrowing side represents a shift in intensity in terms of relationship, and the products become increasingly of a commodity nature. Bonds come close to equity in terms of sensitive information, but the chief executive is likely to have less direct involvement. However, the house involved will have cultivated links at this level because the chief executive will still be concerned to have his/her company associated only with finance houses of 'appropriate stature'. There is also, as with equity, the problem of public visibility. The failure of a bank syndication is not, however, as dramatic for a company's image as something that fails in public markets; especially today when these may be spread across the globe.

Borrowings by syndication will generally be managed entirely out of the company's treasury department with the CEO perhaps being wheeled out only for the signing ceremony. Relationship issues here are a little more diffuse, depending on the purpose of the funding and the frequency that the borrower comes to market. The treasurer will often be concerned to 'reward' banks that have remained close to the company by ensuring that the lead bank invites the other relationship banks. Whether this is necessarily seen as a reward by the invitees is another matter, depending on the pricing and terms; and this is often the time when there is a ritual reassessment of the relationship in the bank. These invitations are generally viewed as important steps in the bank towards more meaningful relationships, but few banks establish much clarity and discipline around the true benefits of this step and its future implications.

The treasurer can generally experiment (within limits) with the plum job of leading a syndicate, much more so than at the equity or bond level, and this keeps the other banks interested because this is the job they all want. There is a broad spectrum of capable players in this area and the treasurer will want to ensure a good cross-section of banks in the 'inner sanctum', membership of which is seen as a quantum step up the relationship ladder.

As for other borrowings, these have tended to become peripheral. With an oversupply of short term credit in the 1980s, most treasurers had no problem in picking up bilateral lines of credit and money market lines, for 'general corporate purposes'. The importance of these lines tends to wax and wane according to the economic climate. This situation changed quite dramatically in the latter part of 1990 with the withdrawal of banks through lack of profitability, capital, or both. This highlighted the need for treasurers to know what their options are when certain sources of supply dry up. It was certainly a time when treasurers looked to what they thought were their relationship banks. Some years on, certain banks are once again asking themselves whether it is sensible to supply credit at current levels. This concern has focused the attention of banks on developing reliable methods of calculating the true profitability of products they sell, in particular credit. Faced with the capital crises and BIS requirements of recent years, banks are paying more attention to the threats of capital erosion. The author's own bank has developed an actuarily-based pricing model for loans which calculates expected losses based on historical loss trends and the risk rating of a company, giving a risk adjusted return on equity (not simply the asset) for the deal. This is a big step forward from the past, but still only one of the tools. In itself it still does not define the value of a relationship.

The lesson of 1990 should be remembered by banks and corporates: in critical times the unthinkable happens. Many banks, faced with their own problems, cancelled treasury lines – the peripheral service, the commodity product with low added value. However, with the disappearance of many other sources of finance they had become very critical, particularly for those companies that did not provide a backstop through committed bank lines. On the other side, there were many banks ruing the day when they became committed members of multi option facilities (MOFs) at margins that lost money. Again, the bankers did not draw some obvious conclusions; if a standby is drawn it will probably be in times and circumstances which reflect disruptions in other markets or the company's fortunes and, almost certainly, these circumstances will call for margins that are higher than those seen in the good times. But all of these facilities were priced in buoyant markets, reflecting conditions at the time, and not those likely to pertain when the facility needed to be used.

The main inescapable conclusion to be drawn here is that, up to 1990, many treasurers had seen their principal objective to be one linked in some way to the bottom line. The reality is that the objective above all others must be to ensure that the company has access to appropriate funding at all times. Anything less than this can precipitate the collapse of the organisation when it is going through difficult times. Many corporate crises can be survived, given time and breathing space. Some have not because the banks were not behind them. The type of relationship required did not exist.

The events of the early years of the 1990s have therefore crystallised a fundamental relationship issue: whereas banks which help companies raise equity and public debt need to know their customers very well in order to exploit the *good times*, banks which lend money directly need to know their customers perhaps even better in order to help in the *bad times*, and this is a much more difficult task. In reality very few commercial banks know their clients well; they are thus often 'fair weather friends'. Apart from a few, the majority that deal with a company have a fairly superficial relationship. It rarely goes much beyond the relationship manager and the treasurer, with occasional lunches between more senior people. (Note, however, that the relationship manager has long been regarded as the linch pin). The reality is that, within commercial banks, the primary responsibility generally lies with a relatively junior employee – unlike investment banks. This is inadequate to handle the difficult situations: the type, for example, where significant debt restructurings are required in order to ensure survival.

Here the decision in the bank to become or stay involved inevitably escalates to senior levels, and if these people do not know the company and its management it is often difficult for them to take the kind of decision that may endanger their own careers. It is often only at this stage that the bank discovers just how superficial its knowledge is, not only of the company's operations but also its competition and the markets in which it operates.

An important recent development in helping to establish the 'mutuality' of a relationship has been the process of detailed account planning in banks, and the sharing of this activity with the client. Again, there are many variations on this theme, and some attempts at these plans are not worth the paper they are printed on. But done well, they can be a vital channel of communication in creating efficiencies, understanding and trust between the parties. Clearly it calls for considerable honesty and many relationship managers and companies are extremely nervous of 'revealing all'. But of course this is a fear which is entirely illogical; if there are 'nasties' in there and truths that must be faced, then the sooner the better. All levels of both the bank and the client must be involved in this process, from the board down. In various ways they are all involved in 'delivering' their side of the agreement, and it is vital in reinforcing and building trust that each side knows who is accountable for what and that they accept this accountability. It is a very useful tool for continuously validating the basis for the relationship and thereby avoiding future surprises.

Perhaps the greatest lesson learned from the 1980s is that when it comes to the crunch and assistance is critical in the funding area, you need to know who your friends are, rather than just your acquaintances.

Operational services

The 'back office' services provided by banks are probably the least glamorous but among the most important they offer. They go largely unseen: not for the back office the collage of tombstones recording famous deals done; not for those bank employees the long weekend at the Spanish golf club resort billed as a brainstorming session. But back office services come high in the relationship spectrum. They are also a vast consumer of expenditure on computer technology.

Increasingly, such services require higher levels of skill and not just at the management level. Two examples will illustrate this trend. Deal matching systems are getting rid of much of the tedious confirmation paperwork and most time is now spent on exceptions for which higher calibre staff are needed. High calibre staff are also needed to understand and settle derivatives trading. Thus the term 'back office' with its Cinderella overtones is giving way to 'operations' which may in some instances include global custody.

The service provided may include some or all of the following.

Payment/settlement services

This may include cheque clearing, electronic transfers (e.g. BACS and CHAPS in the UK), foreign exchange settlements, letters of credit, payroll and cash services, and so on. This is an area where great attention to detail is required and where there is considerable scope for misunderstanding between bank and client. Most of the day-to-day business with a company is concerned with routine transactions and relationships soon go sour when the company feels that basic business needs are not being properly attended to. It does not require great imagination to hear the client say 'If you can't get the simple things right, how can we trust you with the big issues?' Conversely, a bank which scores heavily in the administration area will often have a head start in being awarded bigger and more lucrative transactions. A bank, therefore, ignores the importance of this service at its peril. In recent years, banks have come to recognise that this area requires high quality management if it is to be run efficiently. It is also one where the risk element has grown with increasing volumes of payments traffic, often involving many payment centres and currencies. Thus 'operational risk' management has become almost as important as credit risk in many banks and, with this, the integrity of the relationship with the client has also become an increasingly important factor.

Information services

This used to involve simply statements of activity transacted but with the development of electronic delivery systems the banks are using these systems to deliver other 'nice to have' as well as essential services. It is these new delivery systems that have characterised this area as a service in its own right, sometimes paid for as a separate item rather than being part of the overall payments services. The classic service is the cash monitoring and control system with many banks offering systems with brand names. There are now so many systems to choose from – and not just from banks – that they are already something of a commodity. From the bank's viewpoint it is often a relationship anchor because companies are not happy to change from one system to another unless the current system is radically deficient.

Custodial services

This is an area which has developed much in recent years with the widening of geographical markets, instruments accessible to investors and recognition by banks that clients will pay for a good all-round service. The information services linked to this area are critical and, arguably, without them, there is no product. Large scale investors – including large companies – have to know instantly and accurately what they own and where it is. The ability to move quickly is essential. So experience on the part of the bank as well as mastery of high technology is vital. Knowledge of settlement procedures in different markets is critical if misunderstandings are to be avoided and cash flows optimised. There have been many traumas in this business in recent years as dealers and investors were carried away by enthusiasm for the new opportunities offered by wider global markets, only to find that their respective back offices had failed to keep up with them.

The key service issues with operational products are as follows:

(a) *Capacity.* An obvious point perhaps, but the ability to handle everything that is thrown at the bank is crucial given that one failed payment can be very expensive as well as embarrassing. This is a size issue as well as one of expertise, although this latter aspect does not generally extend to very much in the way of creativity or inventiveness: rather the priority is reliability.
(b) *Reliability.* In processing any item, accuracy is vital. There is no merit in adding bells and whistles which attempt to dress up the service as something different from the competition unless they contribute to greater efficiency; and, within that efficiency, lower cost per item does not count if accuracy is compromised. Faster does not necessarily mean better. This is a process that goes on

all day, every day of the year and the potential for chaos is enormous if things do not work consistently as they are supposed to.

(c) *Security.* The potential for fraud in this area is ever present. Confidence that the bank's systems are thief-proof is very important. None are, of course, but the ability to demonstrate that this risk has been minimised, especially with the newer computer-based systems, is important.

Of secondary importance to these points therefore are cost and sophistication. However, the problem in establishing a new relationship and displacing an entrenched competitor, is that the sales proposition is usually heavily based on these secondary issues. The only thing that new competitors can prove in an absolute sense to the client is that they will charge less for their services, and they have more bells and whistles. Demonstrating capacity, reliability and security takes time.

The crucial importance of these services to good relationships

The trust that is built up between a treasurer and the bank in these areas is one based on being able to sleep at night and not being distracted from more important tasks by endless trivia. These relationships do not change frequently because it is too difficult to do so. The scale, in terms of volume and variety of items being handled, makes change a potentially messy business with the prospect of sleepless nights for some time to come. So the relationships tend to become locked in. Given a satisfactory level of service such relationships are only reviewed on a three to five year cycle basis. They can be compared to the relationship between companies and audit firms.

However, this can give rise to complacency on both sides. The bank knows the treasurer has limited options, at least in the short term; so the incentive to 'volunteer' improvements in efficiency and provide enhancements to existing services is not there to the same extent as in other areas.

If a competitor offers lower costs the existing bank can usually counter this sufficiently to see off the intruder. This will not always involve matching exactly the new terms, rather enough to blunt the incentive for change. Indeed, treasurers will often use the competitive offers deliberately as a stick with which to threaten their banks, knowing that there is little likelihood that they will carry out the threat, but enough to bring the incumbent bank back, near enough, into line.

On the treasurer's side, the prospect of restructuring this area is a daunting one. It is not only large and complex (in terms of volume of detail), but many treasurers still do not feel technically competent in this area; expertise is often limited. Also, it is often very difficult to establish the real added value of many of the new computer-based service improvements. There is often no alternative but to employ an outside consultant to assist in this evaluation process, to provide not only expertise but also objectivity.

There is no doubt that in many companies there is significant untapped potential for service improvements which lead directly to lower costs and enhanced revenues; and in the global markets in which companies now operate, where timeliness of information and speed of action can significantly impact costs and income, computerised delivery systems have an increasingly critical role. Hence the attractiveness of custodial services which offer an all-inclusive cost to the customer and to the bank's solid annuity income.

Investigating this area usually involves getting to the heart of not only *what* the company does for its business, but also *how* it does it. Many surprising items often surface as a result. One treasurer of a major UK corporation discovered significant inefficiencies in the company's purchasing function as a consequence of just such an investigation and was duly rewarded with being made head of purchasing; perhaps not a move he had been looking for!

From the bank relationship viewpoint, the process is difficult and prolonged. Clearly, the treasurer cannot switch suppliers frequently, so breaking in is difficult. But if a bank is truly serious about long term relationships and has the necessary capabilities, this presents an important opportunity, especially as they know many of the present relationships have not seriously been reviewed for some time and must therefore have weaknesses which can be highlighted and exploited.

Some years ago, a major US bank, when going through a difficult period, was faced with the problem of how to maintain relationships with clients in the traditional product areas when these clients were increasingly concerned about declining debt ratings for the bank from the agencies. Ratings are often used by treasurers to determine which banks should remain in the 'inner sanctum' of key relationship banks. In order to maintain relationships the bank switched the emphasis to operational services.

The critical issue was lack of credibility in this area, since there was no historic track record. The psychology was therefore important. Any sales proposition that implied an immediate full service capability was likely to fail. Also any step, however small, which required some form of 'locking in' was also likely to be unacceptable; for example, the provision of services which required the customer to effect some form of computer link with the bank.

The bank chose to sell first a stand-alone treasury workstation whose principal purpose was to assist in the administration of treasury operations. In an increasingly diverse financial world, with an ever widening range and complexity of products, one of the major tasks facing a treasurer is simply to keep track of events. Use of the product did not require any interaction with the bank (other than for training and software updates) so the treasurer felt able to take this step without feeling any commitment necessarily to go further.

However, if the product proved successful the bank had achieved an important step. It had gained some credibility in the area of applying technology to the treasury function in a way that added value. Consequently, any further propositions about using technology would be likely to have a more ready ear and higher levels of confidence with the treasurer concerned. As a result, the relationship could be built gradually by a series of confidence building steps, and a bank which had 'run out of goods' in one area, was able to rebuild the relationship in a new area.

Foreign exchange and money trading

The dealing room has come to epitomise the ultimate form of product driven selling and generally is felt to represent a pure commodity where banks are differentiated only on price.

There is more than just an element of truth in this. Contact for this type of business is inevitably by telephone and, therefore, the 'arm's length' nature of transactions is emphasised. Little of the business is formalised by documentation and, where it exists, there is generally the caveat that any limits are on an uncommitted basis and business can be stopped at any time at the sole discretion of the bank. Not what you would call a warm and cosy arrangement. Equally, from the company's perspective, a firm line is taken in marking limits for bank counterpart exposures, usually based on the bank's debt rating which, in some cases, will exclude them entirely from the list of acceptable suppliers. This is an interesting relationship issue in that banks are expected to continue supporting their clients in difficult times, but the reverse obligation clearly does not yet exist. It is not enough to say that banks are in the risk business and, generally, their clients are not. We are all in risk businesses and if relationships have any value they will acknowledge the need to be there, within reason, for the other party in a variety of climates.

The intensity of competition in the foreign exchange area has driven the straightforward contracts into the area of being a commodity. There are many suppliers but, in selecting those with whom a company will deal, relationship issues do play a role. The fact that the bank may already provide services in other areas may help but often it is the other way around. Many banks use this product area as a toe in the door – the first step in providing a broader range of services. Clearly, the treasurer needs to be comfortable that those other steps are credible ones. Nevertheless, this is a very easy way to 'test out' certain characteristics of a bank without getting locked in. As a service area it is the complete antithesis of operational services; the treasurer can virtually jump in and out at will. Recent developments have shown the usefulness of linking straightforward foreign exchange transactions to the custodial service where one exists. In this way, 'commodity' deals can become part of the service relationship and hence less of a 'commodity'.

What the treasurer can learn will be limited and confined to events over a fairly short period of time. In driving prices to a bare minimum, companies have to accept that banks also have the right to terminate services at will, when terms are no longer acceptable to them. However, it is possible to learn something about the relative styles of each counterparty, and the provision of any service provides a conduit through which to develop other ideas with which to broaden the relationship.

At the personal level, strong links are often developed between the relevant dealing staff in the two organisations which modifies, to some extent, the pure commodity element of these links. In addition, treasurers usually lean towards those institutions where they value the quality of advice being given. In this fast moving and complex area, where no one has a monopoly on useful knowledge, this can be a key support for the treasurer.

In that sense, the commodity element of treasury services is also being countered by the development of derivative products linked to the concept of 'financial risk management'. Derivatives can broaden the capabilities of companies to take a truly proactive and more diversified approach in managing, rather than reacting to, the risks thrown up by the increasingly international and thereby uncertain nature of their businesses. Competitive differentiation, therefore, can come through either the ability to offer more esoteric products, or advice on how to apply them to risk management, or both. In this latter respect it is interesting how some banks have successfully used this area as the major building block in their relationships by acting as an adviser to their clients rather than simply a supplier, and backing the client in a way that would not have been possible before.

All in all, therefore, the treasury area can be one where the relationship is very active and very busy as regards 'plain vanilla', price driven services, but with the potential to disappear quickly (i.e. no strong relationship lock) or it can be a key and stable, if not core element of a relationship if it extends to true advisory or service status.

Trade finance

Trade finance comes in many guises, from short term factoring of receivables to government-backed export financing, to long term complex trade deals including project financing and so on (depending on your definitions). It would be impossible, and perhaps less than useful, to attempt in this chapter to tackle all of them in terms of relationship implications, but some general points do emerge.

Many people have forecast the demise of short term trade finance as a credible banking service, pointing to the increasing use of open accounting trading. Certainly this is a clear trend between the developed countries, although exporters would do well to look at the statistics for trade defaults and may be surprised at which countries head the list.

Nevertheless, as this trend has increased so has the volume of trade with the more 'exotic' countries of the world, areas in which a treasurer's knowledge of counterparts and trade practices may be very limited. Here a bank can add real value in terms of technical expertise, not possessed by all banks: expertise in documentary credits, operational issues, country knowledge, correspondent banking expertise, and so on.

In spite of its often mundane image this is an area where a bank can make a critical difference to a company's commercial competitiveness. For example, a bank which is prepared to take on country exposure in the form of buyer credits and/or has real expertise in how to do business in particular countries which are new to a company, can literally open up new markets for that company and the treasurer may look like a hero to his/her colleagues in the export department.

As a business area it can offer a rich diversity of services for the bank including straightforward credit, government-subsidised funding, foreign exchange, letters of credit, performance bonds, payment services, and so on. It is this diversity and the relatively limited competition that helps to 'lock in' a supplier who has provided reliable service over a long period of time. Consequently frequent switching of suppliers is less common and, therefore, breaking in is difficult for a new competitor.

But here too, complacency can lead to inefficiencies. The fact that it works often leads to a reluctance to tinker with it. For example, in the short term trade area, large sums of money can often be locked up in inefficient payments processes. This can be compounded by poor information systems which fail to alert the treasurer to such inefficiencies.

This is an area where computerised information and payments services are increasingly critical and can add real value by increasing efficiencies of money flow, shortening payments cycles, and so on. However, the bank that has the better operational service may not have the other skills which are important too.

At the longer term end of the operation many of the issues are the same but innovation and creativity generally become more important, and these require local expertise as a base. Time adds complexity, particularly where exotic markets are concerned, if only because the uncertainty factor can become almost exponential! For example, longer term foreign exchange cover may not be possible because the markets simply do not exist. Here the range of banks that can help narrows rapidly, and a company may be forced to use a particular bank simply because it is the only one that can do that type of business. Such a situation would be rare in the extreme, but it behoves any treasurer to ensure that at least one of the company's core banks is capable of providing service in this area if it is contemplating regular business in these types of territories.

Generally, trade finance represents a very strong relationship services area, where banks can truly differentiate themselves and add real value to the treasury function. Although much of the old mystique is being removed and terms of trade are becoming much simpler around the world, it is a field where the scale and diversity can lead to sleepless nights if it does not work properly and consistently.

Conclusions

It would be possible to subdivide banking into even more groupings, but the areas discussed in this chapter are useful in focusing the relationship issues and demonstrating a number of points.

The idea of a banking relationship is fraught with definitional problems but at the heart of it there must be more than just a dialogue. At the very least it requires mutual trust and understanding, followed by some 'goods' that produce a measurable benefit for both sides.

The ability to sustain an obvious competitive advantage in banking services is increasingly difficult at the purely mechanical level; however, the overlay of trust based on demonstrated performance is critical. But the acid test in today's intensely competitive environment is much more to do with hard dollars and cents and less to do with knives and forks.

But the whole is inevitably the sum of various moving parts and the speed at which they change will depend to what extent the suppliers can demonstrate superior added value. For a spot foreign exchange transaction this may simply be the price on the day; for a complex range of operational services it may take months, if not years of work to prove the benefits. The important point is that it is never a static process; it has to be worked at constantly. The basis for the relationship must continually be validated on both sides.

Many relationships have become purely social ones because people have failed to recognise this point and when realisation dawns it can come as something of a shock.

During the 1980s there were many who felt that the role, particularly of traditional banks and banking services was diminishing to an almost peripheral level of importance in the context of a company's financing needs. This was compounded by the reluctance of many banks to recognise and respond to market changes. So much of banking strategies reflected wishful thinking rather than realistic interpretations of events, and this was often reflected in their relationships with clients.

The recessionary environment of the early 1990s should have concentrated everyone's minds on the need to bring realism to the relationship process and establish where there continue to be goods to be traded. Are the bankers your lenders of last resort – and do they know it?

3 Relationships in investment banking

As we saw in Chapter 1, significant changes are taking place in investment banking. These changes are likely to continue on a global basis, essentially driven by competitive pressures. On the one hand, international commercial banks such as Hong Kong and Shanghai, Deutsche, JP Morgan and Swiss Bank Corporation have concluded that lending at low margins to major companies as a main business is not sensible. On the other, investment banks have seen that the only way to gain and retain major clients is to have access to large amounts of capital. United States investment banks such as Merrill Lynch began to follow this trend some years ago, either seeking well capitalised partners or going public, although interestingly, Goldman Sachs decided to remain a partnership following the very profitable year in 1995.

Thus investment banking is becoming a global one-stop business. Mergers, acquisitions, equity and bond issues, placing power and special products – all are taken for granted by larger companies. Whether this trend entirely suits the corporate customer is a moot point. Companies require quality advice and the ability to deliver big numbers, but they also like strong and continued relationships especially in sensitive areas involving the corporate strategy. These relationships will often be personal and as teams or individuals see themselves as global players, clients are either moving from one institution to another, or increasingly, dipping into the expertise of more than one bank.

This chapter explains the services available from investment banks. As with commercial banks, these services are not available from all banks; indeed some have chosen to remain niche players believing that they still play an important role by doing so. The two centres of investment banking are New York and London. In New

York it began through a series of mergers, takeovers and incorporation, so as to offer a total advisory service to clients together with the capability of using the bank's own capital for position taking, risk assumption or speculation. From this stemmed the need for products that laid off risk and led to the growth in derivatives. In London, the process began with a revolution in 1986 called 'Big Bang' which brought together two previous and separate sides of investment banking, namely stockbrokers and stock-jobbers – market makers. Commercial banks were allowed to buy into these functions and there followed a rush to build all-round banking businesses led by US banks. This initial rush was often as ill thought out as it was sudden and it took several years before clear trends became established. It is only now that something near the final picture is emerging with the market dominated by a few commercial/investment banks supported by highly skilled niche players.

While New York and London represent the core of global and investment banking, it does not mean that the action is dominated by US and British banks. It is now true to say that London is more of a European investment banking centre since major non-British European banks have acquired a substantial stake in investment banking.

In describing the services available in investment banking we use the example of Kleinwort Benson. Kleinwort Benson was always a big UK merchant bank and then during the 1986 changes opted to take the so-called 'integrated' route, by buying Grievson Grant, a stockbroker, and Charlesworth, a stock-jobber (market maker), thus making itself an investment bank competing with others such as Goldman Sachs, Salomon Brothers and Merrill Lynch. In 1995, believing it lacked sufficient amounts of capital, required for success in investment banking nowadays, it agreed to a friendly takeover by Dresdner Bank, the second largest German bank, which wanted to increase its stake in London and in investment banking.

Integrated investment banking services

Kleinwort Benson is one of a number of large investment banks with headquarters in London. Its peer group includes Deutsche Morgan Grenfell, SBC Warburg and Schroders. Other major investment banks, notably from the US, also have a significant presence in London. London has the right financial infrastructure to support these activities which are increasingly global.

It will be readily apparent that the style and perception of different banks varies considerably. An insider would probably identify two styles:

(a) Traditional UK-style relationship merchant bank; and
(b) US-style transaction-oriented investment bank.

Again some caution is required with such stereotypes. The US house Goldman Sachs is certainly one that would see itself as a relationship bank.

The increase in competition for business has prompted the UK-style bank to develop a more proactive style of marketing. However, as yet, they do not have a reputation for the aggressive transaction-oriented marketing shared by their US counterparts. Part of the reason for the different approaches lies in the differing nature of banking styles, but part also is due to the fact that the US banks do not have an indigenous UK franchise. Thus they have to win each piece of business by differentiating themselves, usually on a product basis, from the rest of the competition. In contrast, UK banks pride themselves on being relationship banks, maintaining ongoing relationships with clients over the long term. As the US banks build up their presence in Europe, they are increasingly aware of the value of relationship banking. Differences in style are also likely to decline as ownership of banks becomes more international and senior bankers move freely from one bank to another.

Corporate finance

Within Kleinwort Benson, corporate finance covers a wide range of advisory work for UK and international clients. The range of activities includes:

(a) General ongoing advice;
(b) Equity and equity-related origination, including international capital markets issues;
(c) Debt advice and origination;
(d) Privatisation;
(e) UK and cross-border mergers and acquisitions (M&A); and
(f) Project finance.

As with other banks, the trend is towards an increasingly international focus, assisted by the establishment of a network of overseas offices. This trend is likely to intensify following the merger with Dresdner Bank which itself has a strong international client base.

The nature of the advisory work undertaken, which is often commercially and market sensitive, means that the corporate finance division has relationships at the highest level with the client. Often, the personal rapport between senior management at the bank and the chairman or chief executive of the client is the key factor in the relationship with the client as a whole. On a day-to-day basis, the most common point of contact is usually the finance director or corporate development director.

Increasing competition has ended the traditionally exclusive nature of the advisory role of a client's merchant bank. This means that the finance director can expect to receive frequent calls from a number of investment banks. The relationship with the individual finance director, understanding his/her needs and position *vis-à-vis* the rest of the board, are key in distinguishing one bank from its competitors.

Financing

Investment banks are not primarily lenders to corporate clients, although UK merchant banks used to supplement bank lending largely to underpin a relationship. This activity has declined in relative importance as corporate loan demand has increased for longer maturities and only large commercial banks can satisfy it.

Instead, the UK banks prefer to concentrate on structuring and arranging syndicated finance as well as specialist operations such as the financing of export credit, leasing and management buyouts. The range of financing within each bank is considerable and the divisions will pride themselves on the development of new innovatively structured products. Convertible capital bonds and joint debenture issues for a group of issuers (such as small brewers and housing associations) are examples of recent products developed.

The separation between corporate finance and financing often disappears when advice on methods of fundraising is given to a client.

The primary point of contact will be the finance director or, in a large organisation, the treasurer. The terms of a particular deal or the technology involved are usually key to winning the business or at least to becoming a member of the panel of banks which are called upon to pitch for business on a regular basis. A reputation for innovative structuring of finance and competitive terms may well be more influential with clients than personal rapport with the individuals at the bank. However, where a panel of banks exists, a good relationship with the clients as well as competitive terms will be necessary.

Securities

In investment banks, the traditional roles of broker and market maker in equity securities, derivatives and corporate bonds are covered as well as the distribution of new and secondary issues to institutional clients. The firm also provides a research service to these clients on specific companies, markets and the general economic outlook.

The clients of the securities division are the institutional fund managers who deal through Kleinwort Benson and rely on the research analysts and the salespeople to provide a knowledgeable view of the company. Through their research work, the analysts build up close relationships with the companies which they cover. It is vital to their work for the analysts to be able to understand the companies' strategy so that this can be conveyed to the investors.

Treasury

At Kleinwort Benson the treasury function covers the following areas as well as general strategy advice and money management services:

(a) *Money market.* Deposit taking and advice on interest rates.
(b) *Foreign exchange.* Comprehensive range of spot and forward foreign exchange services and currency options.
(c) *Derivative products.* Derivative products such as swaps, forward rate agreements (FRAs), interest rate options and advice on interest rates, risk management and hedging strategies.
(d) *Government debt.* Gilt-edged market makers and dealing service in European government debt.
(e) *Non-government.* Includes sterling bonds and floating rate notes debt.

For most clients, the important factors in selecting which banks to use on a treasury transaction will be the terms and structure of the proposed transaction along with the best advice. A good relationship with the finance director or the treasurer (if one exists) will be important in winning the business and clients appreciate the trust that develops between them and the bank over the course of a few transactions.

The increasingly sophisticated number of products available means that clients sometimes contact a bank they know well for impartial advice, regardless of whether the bank is providing the product. The bank providing the general advice will be used because the client trusts it for its independent advice.

Investment management

Investment management ranges from fund management for the largest of pensions funds, through to looking after an individual's personal portfolio. Under Securities and Investments Board (SIB) rules, there must be a Chinese wall separating investment management from the other operations of the bank. (The term 'Chinese wall' has been adopted to describe the process whereby knowledge of deals such as mergers or acquisitions is not allowed to be communicated before it becomes public, to parts of the bank which could profit from the knowledge; it is a term used internationally).

In fact, all the fund management arms of the UK investment banks operate a strict independence policy from the other operations. There are, therefore, few opportunities for a relationship that has developed within the investment management division to be generally used in the rest of the bank. The close relationships that are established between the fund managers and their clients, institutional and private, are based on trust and performance record and are not intended to be covered further in this chapter.

Developing relationships

Investment banks in the UK pride themselves on their relationship style of banking. The relationship with the clients is built up over many years, often decades, generating trust on both sides. The bank has seen the client's business through different business cycles and is able to understand its essential dynamics. The relationship is cemented by the completion of different transactions at various stages of the company's development.

The best adviser is one who can be relied upon for sound and mature judgement, to tell hard truths when necessary, and to give an unbiased, independent view. The question of independence goes to the heart of professional integrity, such that the adviser should be able to give the best advice for that client, regardless of the profit to the bank associated with a particular course of action. The ultimate sanction if the client does not wish to take the advice and wishes to pursue a course of action which the bank believes is unwise, is to resign as adviser. This may appear a slightly dramatic solution, but it is not as uncommon as may be thought.

The key to the relationship

The key relationship with a client will usually be with the chairman or chief executive. However, the extent to which these individuals are involved in maintaining the relationship with the investment bank usually depends on the size and style of the client company. It is quite common in the largest of corporates for the finance director to be the main relationship with the bank. This very much depends on the finance director's role within the company and the extent to which he or she is involved in the strategic decision making. If the finance director's role is confined to supervision of the treasury operations he/she will be less important in overall relationship terms to the bank.

The quality of the relationship with the chief executive will be more or less important depending on the style of operation of that individual. Often the chief executive will focus primarily on equity-related matters (a cynic would say anything that affects the share price) and delegate debt-related matters to the finance director or treasurer. In many large companies this debt versus equity division is a strategic split, and in fact reflects the nature of the work involved. On the equity side, there is more emphasis on the quality of service; particularly where this involves ongoing strategic advice. In contrast, on the debt side there is more emphasis on the products – on terms and pricing – and therefore the relationship is generally more focused. Indeed the relationship can continue successfully even where the bank cannot provide all the products the client requires. Of course, if a transaction involving a certain product goes badly wrong or, for example, the product is withdrawn, the relationship with the client suffers.

Within large banks, it is usually the corporate finance division that has the prime contacts at the most senior level. For other divisions, relationships with the client at different levels are more or less important depending on the nature of the service offered. Generally the level of these relationships will be lower than that of the corporate finance division.

Nurturing ongoing relationships

One of the advantages of large investment banks is the ability to service a client through the different stages of its development.

At the most basic level, seed or development equity capital can be provided to enable private companies to expand. This can be combined with debt finance, although most banks are now seeking to arrange the finance rather than provide it.

As the company grows, other forms of finance might be appropriate, such as export credit or leasing arrangements, or treasury operations.

When the company is of a sufficient size to consider tapping wider capital markets, the bank will be able to offer advice as to how to expand further. This may be by floating on the domestic stock market, or by a private placement of equity with long term institutional shareholders. Alternatively, the corporate finance department may be able to assist in finding a trade partner who would be willing to make an investment in the company or acquire it outright.

As the company expands, it can benefit from the wider range of services available from the bank, as well as the advisory relationships built up over the years. The bank's wide variety of services combined with an international spread of operations should match the aspirations of the most ambitious client.

Marketing

The way in which an investment bank markets its services to clients and potential clients will often depend on the size of the organisation. It will also reflect the image that the bank wishes to project based on the character of the senior individuals responsible for the major accounts.

In the largest banks, relationship managers may exist to look after the needs of all the bank's clients and potential clients. Often senior directors are responsible for co-ordinating the whole of the bank's resources to service the needs of the client. They should possess a good knowledge of the individual needs and strategy of each client under their care. While not expert in all the services provided by their banking colleagues, they should be able to orchestrate the resources of the whole bank in order to serve the client and to profit the bank. Readers will recognise the similarity of this side to that of an account officer in a commercial bank, except that the account officer is rarely so senior (see Chapter 2, p. 16).

As an alternative to relationship managers, a bank may have directors who are responsible for particular clients and potential clients, but who also spend part of their time on key transactions for those clients. An advantage of this system is that an involvement in transactions for the client will give the manager an in-depth understanding of the client's business and at the same time reassure the client that its usual contact is in control of its important or sensitive deal.

The most aggressive banks, usually US, have led the way in marketing by seeking to win clients away from the UK banks. It is fair to say that this competition on home ground has taken some UK banks by surprise. Their reaction has been to start to market their services to their existing clients as well as to target clients.

In order to keep their existing advisers on their toes, some clients have started to require a pitch to be made for each piece of new business. The existing relationship bank will then have to present its credentials along with its competitors. This can lead to an erosion of the trust on which the advisory relationship is based and probably should not be employed as a tactic unless the existing bank is deficient in the services it provides.

Sources of marketing initiatives

It is not possible any longer to rely solely on traditional transactions skills to win business. Clients now expect a bank to understand their business and the markets in which they operate. Both the financial markets in which the bank operates and the clients it seeks to serve are international. Most clients expect their banks to have operational capacity in the major markets overseas.

Industry specialisation enables a bank to target accurately its clients' needs, especially in the area of corporate finance. The best advisers are not necessarily those who have 'hands on' experience of a particular industry; rather, they understand the strategic objectives of the clients within their markets and hence the appropriate advice and financing for their requirements.

An international spread of operations, combined with an in-depth knowledge of a sector, enable a bank to offer enhanced acquisition and financing advice. This is particularly useful for advising clients on transactions outside the clients' normal geographical area.

Why use a particular investment bank?

The skills required to retain a client are often different from those needed to win business. However, the reasons for using a particular bank could be summarised into the three Ps:

(a) People.
(b) Perception.
(c) Products.

To retain existing clients, personal relationships with the individual contacts at the banks are probably the most important. Clients are only human and it is natural that they prefer to deal with people with whom they have developed a rapport. It is always easier to seek advice on a formal or casual basis from an individual with whom one shares a common view. In addition, a long stressful transaction can be made more bearable by a good working relationship between banker and client. A close relationship with key individuals can enable the adviser to impart hard truths to the client, where necessary.

Perception is the perception or reputation of the particular bank. Some of this will inevitably come through the representation of the bank in the media, which to a large extent is dependent on the effectiveness of the corporate publicity machine. Certain areas of the bank, such as corporate finance or treasury, will be particularly affected by the wider public perception.

The other major factor affecting a client's perception of a bank is inevitably the client's own experience of its dealings with the individuals at the bank. Word of mouth in a relatively small community like the City of London still counts for a great deal. The cross-connections of executive and non-executive directors on the boards of all major UK corporates provide a network of opinion on particular banks and individual bankers. Sometimes directors have current or historic connections to particular investment banks, perhaps through having worked at the bank concerned.

However, to win new business in the current competitive marketplace, the order of importance of the three Ps is different. The particular product being offered becomes key to distinguishing between various banks. In addition to the product, the general reputation of the bank and the chemistry between the client and banker will be important. The new client, with no knowledge of the individuals at the bank, will be impressed by the skills displayed by the banker in terms of familiarity with the product and the client's industry sector as well as the general importance of the client to the bank.

The first question to ask when considering how to manage a relationship with an investment bank is to analyse exactly what you require the bank to do. This involves considering such matters as the level of service required, which would include the seniority of the people on the team and the commitment in terms of time to be given.

Thereafter, the relationship is built on the trust established between the principal contacts at the bank and the client. To a large extent, trust is created by a good communication flow between the two parties. Like all relationships, the most common cause of difficulties is a failure in communication. The more the banker knows about the client's business and aims, the more he or she will be able to tailor the bank's products to the client's requirements. The most efficient way of operating is for the client to think of the bank's team as part of the client's own group.

4 Legal and regulatory aspects of banking

Background

To the non-banker and to any corporate user of banking services, the important legal and regulatory aspects of banking are: the way in which they influence what services banks can provide; the way in which they provide reassurance about the financial strength of banks; how they impact on the cost of the services; and how they afford protection to the client on key relationship issues, such as confidentiality, conflict of interest and similar matters.

The developments in banking regulation in many of the world's major financial markets in recent years have been much influenced by: the increasing internationalisation of banking markets; the increasing competitive pressures among banks; the process of disintermediation with much of the banks' traditional business being taken over by the capital markets; and the move by banks into other areas such as the securities industry.

The banking industry is sometimes seen by outsiders as conservative and even boring. Such a perception on the evidence since the mid-1980s is well wide of the mark. Innovation has been a key characteristic of the industry over this period. Globalisation and the resulting increased competition have been the driving forces behind this development. For the regulator, keeping pace with innovation has become difficult. To match the globalisation, regulators are seeking global solutions. But necessarily such solutions can only be compromises, given the widely differing regulatory and commercial structures in the various major banking markets.

Before the international pressures of globalisation were relevant, regulation was mainly influenced by the varied domestic concerns of the different markets, including financial disasters. In the United States for example, the banking collapses of the early 1930s resulted in the passing of the Glass-Steagall Act which sought to separate commercial and investment banking. Prior to that, the McFadden Act of 1927 prohibited federally-chartered banks from establishing branches across state lines. Within states the rules differed. To this day there is no true national bank in the United States and there are still over 12 000 banks. But the movement in recent years has been towards easing these restrictions and the Riegle-Neal Inter-State Banking and Branching Efficiency Act of 1994 gives new powers to establish branches and to conduct business across state lines.

In Japan there has been a high degree of specialisation between banks. Long term has been separated from short term finance, trust from commercial and banking from securities activities. Here too, these precise lines are being eroded by deregulation.

By contrast, the continent of Europe has never understood the need to separate commercial and investment banking; 'universal' banking is the norm and forms the basis of the European Union's Second Banking Directive (see below).

These trends towards a relaxation of the regulatory climate are the exact reverse of the experience in the United Kingdom. Historically, the UK has been a country with loose to non-existent legal constraints, but an unofficial and largely effective system of informal controls. But events since the mid-1970s and the processes of globalisation have influenced a major series of changes, leading to the introduction of a panoply of statutory regulations and control. We have therefore used the UK as a case study for the development and implementation of a tight regulatory system.

Since 1979 the UK has introduced a whole series of regulations governing finance and banking, so that from being a country with an unofficial but largely effective climate of control it now has the most rigorous formal regulatory system.

As a result of these developments, the regulatory regime applicable to banks in the UK and elsewhere has had to adapt to a rapidly changing industry. In the United Kingdom, it has had to do this at the same time as changing from a highly informal, non-legal regime to one that is statute based, and also one which reflects the international requirements not only of the European Union but also the pressures towards broader harmonisation under the auspices of the Bank for International Settlements in Basle.

Before 1979 there was no statutory basis for any regulation of the banking industry as such. It was remarkable, and characteristic of the club nature of the City of London, that despite this lack of a proper legal mandate the Bank of England in practice exercised considerable authority on such questions as who could establish banks in the UK and what services those banks could provide. This authority was exercised by moral suasion or, in the familiar old phrase, by the Governor raising his eyebrows.

Two factors brought this informal system under some pressure. The first was the Secondary Banking Crisis of the mid-1970s. The Bank of England's informal supervision was most effective regarding the major banks, particularly those relying on authorisation under the Exchange Control Act 1947 to engage in foreign exchange business. It was ineffective, or non-existent, in relation to the growing number of smaller banks some of which became heavily involved in the financing of real estate. Problems in the property market and other factors in the early 1970s caused several of these secondary banks to face collapse. The Bank organised a lifeboat rescue and it became clear that the supervision system needed to be extended and strengthened.

The second factor was the UK's admission to the European Community and the move towards harmonisation of banking laws.

The Banking Act 1979 represented the first codification of banking regulation and controls, requiring the authorisation or licensing of any institution accepting deposits and establishing a statutory basis for supervision over all such institutions by the Bank of England.

During the 1980s there were pressures for further change. These pressures included the rescue of Johnson Matthey, a government investigation and new banking legislation – the Banking Act 1987.

The business of banking

The Banking Act 1987 gave the Bank of England important new supervisory powers but retained as its focus the authorisation of deposit taking. The Act's key provision, section 3, makes it an offence for a person to accept a deposit in the course of carrying on a 'deposit taking business' unless authorised to do so by the Bank of England. For the purposes of the Act, a business is a 'deposit taking business' if money received by way of deposit in the course of business is then on-lent or any other business activity is financed out of this deposit. To fall within the Act, the business must hold itself out as accepting deposits on a day-to-day basis; the occasional acceptance of deposits falls outside its scope.

The term 'bank', although not specifically referred to in the Banking Act 1987, has been defined in numerous statutes and at common law (see also Chapter 1). The common law definition was provided in the 1966 case of *United Dominions Trust Ltd* v. *Kirkwood* [1966] 2 QB 431, CA, where it was held that there are three essential characteristics of a banking business : (a) collecting cheques for customers; (b) paying cheques drawn by their customers; and (c) keeping current accounts for their customers. All three characteristics must be satisfied for an institution to be considered a bank at common law.

It may seem anachronistic to describe a bank in these 1966 terms or indeed in terms of 'deposit taking business' as in the 1987 Act. More recognisable, perhaps, is the description of the activities of credit institutions in the Second Banking Directive (89/646/EEC), the main instrument for creating the single market for banking services within the European Union. These activities include:

(a) Acceptance of deposits and other repayable funds from the public.
(b) Lending (including, *inter alia*, consumer credit, mortgage credit, factoring, with or without recourse, and financing of commercial transactions, including forfaiting.
(c) Financial leasing.
(d) Money transmission services.
(e) Issuing and administering means of payment (e.g. credit cards, travellers' cheques and bankers' drafts).
(f) Guarantees and commitments.
(g) Trading for own account or for account of customers in:
    (i)   money market instruments;
    (ii)   foreign exchange;
    (iii)   financial futures and options;
    (iv)   exchange and interest rate instruments;
    (v)   transferable securities.
(h) Participation in share issues and the provision of services related to such issues.
(i) Advice to undertakings on capital structure, industrial strategy and related questions and advice and services relating to mergers and the purchase of undertakings.
(j) Money broking.
(k) Portfolio management and advice.
(l) Safekeeping and administration of securities.
(m)Credit reference services.
(n) Safe custody services.

The most striking feature of this list is the overlap between what used to be considered securities business, the preserve of investment and merchant banks, and 'straight' banking business, generally viewed as lending and deposit taking, the preserve of the commercial banks. Banking activities are those of the universal bank which prevails in Continental Europe, where both core banking activities and other financial services are provided by a single corporate entity.

Bank regulation

The emergence of financial conglomerates whose business includes a wide range of services, including the provision of corporate finance and the selling of insurance products, has had a marked effect on the regulatory structure of the banking market. In the United Kingdom, unlike Continental Europe, supervision and regulation is conducted along functional lines. This has resulted in a number of different authorities being charged with regulating different facets of a bank's business.

The Bank of England regulates much of the activity of UK incorporated banks through the supervision of capital adequacy, the review of prudential returns, and its relationship with bank auditors, as well as its direct interest in the skills of management and the control environment in which banks operate. The Bank has a tiered approach to supervision, its principal tools being the authority delegated to it through the Banking Act itself, the 1993 Statements of Principles (which set out certain criteria regarding authorisation and the implementation of the Second Banking Directive) and a series of policy notices. These policy notices cover a wide range of issues, from accounting records and control systems to loan transfers and securitisation to netting and cash collateral.

In respect of those banks that undertake investment business, this activity is regulated within a complex structure at the head of which is HM Treasury but most of whose functions are delegated to the Securities and Investments Board (SIB), the body set up under the Financial Services Act 1986. If a bank conducts insurance business, the regulatory authority is the Department of Trade and Industry. Also, although deposit taking (and lending) falls within the ambit of the Banking Act 1987, banks which undertake consumer credit business are required to hold a licence to do so under the Consumer Credit Act 1974.

Investment business is regulated under the Financial Services Act. 'Investment' is widely defined in Schedule 1 to the Act and includes: (a) securities; (b) options; (c) futures; (d) long term insurance contracts; and (e) contracts for differences. The activities of dealing in, arranging deals in, managing and advising on investments – as well as the activity of operating collective investment schemes, such as unit trusts – all fall within the Act. Banks wishing to undertake any of these activities are required to join an appropriate self-regulating organisation (SRO), comply with relevant conduct of business rules and satisfy a 'fit and proper test'. The current three SROs are the Securities and Futures Authority (SFA), the Investment Management Regulatory Organisation (IMRO) and the Personal Investment Authority (PIA).

There are exemptions within the Financial Services Act 1986. Under section 43 banks and other institutions included in a list maintained with the Bank of England are exempted from the requirements of the Act in respect of transactions in the London money markets. The regulation of the wholesale markets in sterling, foreign exchange and bullion is carried out by the Bank of England through the media of the Grey Paper and the London Code of Conduct for principals and broking firms in the wholesale markets, the current editions of which are dated December 1995 and July 1995 respectively. Under the Grey Paper a section 43 listed institution must comply with the Code of Conduct and satisfy the Bank of England's 'fit and proper' requirements.

A system of different regulatory authorities for different activities could be viewed as unnecessarily cumbersome and with significant cost disadvantages. In practice, the principle of lead regulation places the Bank of England in control of the financial supervision of UK incorporated banks. The way that this has been achieved is through a series of memoranda of understanding between the SROs and the Bank of England which stipulate that the Bank of England should take responsibility for monitoring the financial position of the banks concerned. Information is shared between regulators; and the relevant SRO's conduct of business rules still apply. Similar arrangements apply to banks incorporated in certain other countries in respect of which lead regulation agreements have been reached between the SIB and/or the Bank of England and the local regulatory authorities.

The 'single passport' and European banking legislation

The United Kingdom supervisory and regulatory regime for the financial services industry, with its emphasis on the functional approach, has been developing at the same time as the international harmonisation of banking laws and practices. In the European Union, the cornerstone legislation, the Second Banking Directive, has as its aim the provision of a 'single licence' for banking 'throughout the Community and the application of the principle of home Member State prudential supervision' (Preamble).

Since 1 January 1993, when the Second Banking Directive was implemented in the United Kingdom, banks or other credit institutions, which are duly authorised as credit institutions in other European member states, have been able to set up a branch in the United Kingdom without the need for local authorisation and subject only to certain notification requirements. In terms of prudential supervision, the home state remains responsible for authorisation, fitness, adequacy of financial resources and prudent manner of operation. The United Kingdom authorities, therefore, retain primary responsibility for the supervision of liquidity of the branches of these credit institutions and exclusive responsibility for the implementation of monetary policy. In respect of UK subsidiaries of overseas credit institutions, these remain subject to United Kingdom rules alone. In relation to credit institutions from outside the European Union: (a) these may operate in the United Kingdom by way of a branch under a United Kingdom banking licence and (b) they may set up a subsidiary in the United Kingdom and apply for a United Kingdom banking licence, thereby gaining the freedom to expand anywhere in the European Union via branches, or to operate on a cross-border basis.

The Second Banking Directive takes an institutional rather than a functional approach, allowing banks to carry out a wide range of activities in member states as set out above. The Directive does not apply to investment firms which are subject to a different supervisory regime and it is for this reason that the Investment Services Directive (93/22/EEC) has been adopted and is being implemented in the member states. The Investment Services Directive aims to complement the Second Banking Directive by creating a separate but equal single licence for non-bank securities businesses. The home member state is to be responsible for the prudential supervision of investment firms, whether or not the firm has a branch in another member state or provides services on a cross-border basis from a branch in one member state to a client in another without physical movement into the client's state. Primary responsibility for conduct of business rules is given to the member state in which the service is provided, the host state. The move to harmonise legislation in the field of banking and financial services has led to the publication (and implementation within member states) of a raft of Directives. These include the Own Funds Directive (89/299/EEC), the Solvency Ratio Directive (89/647/EEC), the Large Exposures Directive (92/121/EEC), the Consolidated Supervision Directive (92/30/EEC), the Money Laundering Directive (91/308/EEC), the Directive on Deposit Guarantee Schemes (94/19/EEC) and the Capital Adequacy Directive (93/6/EEC), as well as the Investment Services Directive noted above.

Capital adequacy

From the perspective of a European corporate, perhaps the most significant regulatory structure to be introduced in the 1990s has been that relating to capital adequacy. Discussions which began in Basle at the Bank for International Settlements (BIS) led to the emergence of the Convergence Agreement in 1988 and were then taken up by the European authorities. The result was the Own Funds, Solvency Ratio and Capital Adequacy Directives. At the same time, the International Organisation of Securities Commissions (IOSCO) was working on a common approach to the question of rules on capital adequacy for securities businesses. The subject remains the focus of debate in the international arena, with various methodologies being suggested for the calculation of market risks. The Basle Committee has issued its amendment to the 1988 Convergence Agreement to deal with these risks and it is considered likely that this will result in an amendment to the Capital Adequacy Directive to allow the use of the latest bank technology.

In the United Kingdom, the Bank of England is responsible for the capital adequacy of UK incorporated authorised institutions. As a result of its rules on consolidation (set out in the Bank of England's 'Notice to Authorised Institutions Implementing the Directive on the Consolidated Supervision of Credit Institutions'), the Bank of England's capital adequacy rules may also affect non-UK incorporated companies because UK institutions must report their capital adequacy positions on a consolidated basis at least twice a year. In its 1993 Statements of Principles the Bank states that 'a key purpose of capital is to provide a stable resource to absorb any losses incurred by any institution and thus protect the interests of depositors and potential depositors.' Capital adequacy is the requirement for banks to maintain sufficient capital to absorb losses in order to protect depositors.

The concept of the capital adequacy regime introduced by Basle is to prescribe a minimum capital requirement for each bank in view of the business entered into by that bank.

The consensus reached in European legislation is to apply the same capital adequacy regime to banks and securities businesses, apart from initial capital requirements (which are higher for banks), assessing the capital requirement in both cases by reference to the nature of the asset that such capital is intended to support. The requirements are calculated differently according to whether they are banking assets or trading assets. The regime applicable to banking assets such as loans derives from the Own Funds and the Solvency Ratio Directives, whereas that applicable to trading assets, essentially those which are tradable and in relation to which a proper market exists, derives from the Capital Adequacy Directive which was implemented in each EU member state as from 1 January 1996.

Under the Own Funds and Solvency Ratio Directives, an institution is essentially required to maintain capital corresponding to a minimum of 8 per cent of the amount of its assets as adjusted to reflect an appropriate risk weighting. At least half of this capital must normally be Tier I capital, broadly adjusted share capital and reserves. Not more than half of the required capital may be in the form of Tier II supplemental capital which includes hybrid capital instruments such as perpetual subordinated debt, and (subject to further limitations) subordinated term debt. The Capital Adequacy Directive has also introduced the concept of Tier III capital, comprising certain subordinated debt and other items not qualifying as Tier II, which can be used as ancillary capital to support a trading book.

The Solvency Ratio Directive (and the Bank of England notice which implements it in the United Kingdom) adopts a system of risk weighting of assets according to the perceived likelihood of counterparty failure. For example, cash and claims on OECD governments and central banks have a 0 per cent weighting (thereby requiring no related capital), whereas unsecured loans to private sector, non-bank borrowers have 100 per cent weighting (requiring minimum capital support of 8 per cent). On-balance sheet items (such as loans which have been advanced) are distinguished from off-balance sheet items (such as a commitment to make a loan, or a bank's obligation under a letter of credit). Off-balance sheet items carry their own 'credit conversion factor' of between 0 per cent and 100 per cent. For example, certain commitments to make advances have a 50 per cent credit conversion factor, thus giving rise to half the capital requirement applicable to the advance itself.

The somewhat crude risk analysis which is implicit in these weightings (such as a reduced weighting of claims on the banking sector as against non-bank borrowers) has been criticised by numerous commentators. It has been pointed out, for example, that

> 'this approach means that, prior to the collapse of BCCI, but at a time when the majority of banks operating actively in the interbank market were sufficiently aware of the problems at BCCI, it was nonetheless cheaper in terms of capital cost for a bank to lend to BCCI than a blue chip corporate.[1]

In practice, banks often structure transactions to use risk weightings efficiently and then use this as a competitive advantage in pricing their transactions.

As has been noted, the Capital Adequacy Directive sets out the rules regarding the risk weighting of assets in the 'trading book'. It also permits institutions to meet lower capital adequacy ratios on this part of their business; by doing so, it acknowledges that less capital is required in respect of a tradable instrument than in respect of an asset which is intended to be held to maturity or for which no market exists. It is therefore conceivable that banks will increasingly attempt to structure their transactions through their 'trading book' and thus provide keener pricing to their customers.

Banker/customer relationship

The relationship between banker and customer has been the focus of particular attention recently as a result of some highly publicised cases in the area of derivatives. Fiduciary duties and the potential for conflicts of interest where different sectors of a bank's business are providing advice to customers are important issues in today's highly competitive business environment.

The basic principle is that a bank owes a duty of confidentiality to its customers. This principle, laid down in the 1924 case of *Tournier* v. *National Provincial and Union Bank of England* (1924) 1KB 461, establishes that the duty of confidentiality between banker and customer is a legal one which arises out of contract, a term being implied into the relationship between a banker and his/her customer that the banker will not divulge to third persons

---

[1]Marc Dassesse, Stuart Isaacs and Graham Penn, *EC Banking Law*, 2nd edition, Lloyd's Commercial Law Library, 1994.

the state of the customer's account, nor the details (or fact) of any dealing between the bank and the customer, nor any information received by the banker as a result of his holding that position. The duty is not an absolute one, being subject to four exceptions: (a) where disclosure is under compulsion of law; (b) where there is a duty to the public to disclose; (c) where the interests of the bank require disclosure; and (d) where disclosure is made with the express or implied consent of the customer.

The scope of the exceptions to the banker's duty of confidentiality remains unclear, with the result that erosion of the duty has occurred, particularly as a result of the enactment of legislation to counter drug trafficking, terrorism and money laundering. Further, the growing use of credit reference agencies and the release of information regarding customers' financial circumstances to them has led to concerns being voiced by consumer groups and calls for legislation to clarify and codify the *Tournier* principles.

In 1992, as a result of a White Paper entitled 'Banking Services: Law and Practice' issued by the government in response to the Jack Report (1989), banking industry associations, the British Bankers' Association, the Building Societies Association, and the Association for Payment Clearing Services released *Good Banking: Code of practice to be observed by banks, building societies and card issuers in their relations with personal customers*. A second edition of the code has since been issued (March 1994). The code includes a section (section 8) headed 'Confidentiality of customer information' which restates the *Tournier* principles without amendment and specifies a procedure for banks giving 'black' or any other information to credit reference agencies. It also requires banks and building societies to comply with the Data Protection Act when obtaining and processing customers' data and to explain to their customers the rights of access under the Data Protection Act to their personal records as held on computer files.

In the context of transactions with sophisticated counterparties, the focus of a number of codes and papers,[2] as well as litigation in both the UK and US courts, has been the legal rights and obligations which arise between parties to financial transactions. In

---

[2]For example: *Transactions in Derivatives – Legal Obligations of Banks to Customers,* a Financial Law Panel Discussion Paper dated May 1995; *Principles and Practices for Wholesale Financial Markets Transactions,* ISDA, August 1995; *Managing Derivatives Risk: A Code of Practice for End-Users of Derivatives*; Futures and Options Associations, December 1995.

the decision of Mance J in *Bankers Trust International Plc* v. *PT Dharmala Sakti Sejahtera* (QBD 1.12.95; [1995] 4 Bank LR 381), the judge noted that the relationship between the two parties, who had entered into derivatives contracts, was not the conventional banker–customer relationship. This was because the bank was 'marketing to existing or prospective purchasers derivative products of its own devising which were both novel and complex' (at p. 392). Duties of an advisory nature should not be too readily implied into such a relationship. The extent of the bank's duty of care was to present accurately and fairly the terms and effects of each of the transactions into which the parties were entering.

The steps that a bank must take in order to fulfil its duty of care to any particular customer will vary according to the level of sophistication of the customer. Each transaction must, therefore, be assessed on its own facts. In this respect, the publication of codes of conduct and practice by various trade associations should assist in ensuring that parties to financial transactions are aware of the duties each has to the other.

Conclusion

Recent years have seen great changes in the structure of the banking and financial services industries, and these changes have necessarily given rise to changes in the legal and regulatory framework within which banking institutions operate. As banks and other financial institutions become active in financial markets which are either new or new to the institutions concerned, there will be increasing pressures on the robustness of the regulatory regimes. Users of banking services and of the financial markets have high expectations about the financial solidity of banks and other market participants and high expectations of standards of integrity. In contrast to this, all financial transactions have elements of risk. The legal and regulatory system must seek to ensure that these risks are managed and that users of the relevant services have appropriate (even if, necessarily, not absolute) protection. But there will be a continuing tension between, on the one hand, the desire to have wide access to the broadest possible range of financial products at the most competitive terms and, on the other, the highest practicable levels of customer protection. The collapse of Barings in early 1995 brought this tension into focus, calling into question the basis on which banks as deposit-taking institutions should be able to participate in the broader range of financial markets. When any financial institution fails, and particularly when that failure is associated with involvement in new markets, there are calls for review of the legal and regulatory structure. It may well be that these factors will be a catalyst for further changes.

5 The place of banking relationships in corporate strategy

Economic history is, in many ways, a history of cycles. Some cycles are sufficiently long for many business people, including bankers, to lack experience of the previous cycle. Because during a full cycle a particular indicator spends most of its time trending either up or down and little of it actually changing direction, many managers grow accustomed to the trend and assume it has become a permanent feature of life. Thus they do not expect a turning point and do not anticipate it even in contingency planning.

The manager who stands out against the trend probably does little for his or her career in the firm – or generally. In banking the effect is as follows. 'A "sound" banker, alas! is not one who foresees danger and avoids it, but one who, when he is ruined, is ruined in a conventional and orthodox way along with his fellows, so that no one can really blame him' (J M Keynes, 'The Consequences to the Banks of the Collapse of Money Values' in *Essays in Persuasion*, 1933.) The same tendency applies in non-financial companies too, however.

Some of this has been at work behind the developments in international banking since the end of the 1960s described in Chapter 1. This chapter is concerned with the place of banking relationships in corporate financial strategy.

Financial strategy

Financial strategy can be seen dynamically as dealing with the risks and relationships between a company's sources of funds and its needs for them. Statically, it can be regarded as balancing the competing claims of providers of finance (which may, of course, include banks) with the assets of the business – at the lowest cost achievable at the point of balance chosen.

A company's financial policy will normally cover:

(a) The total amount of finance drawn in relation to its ordinary shareholders' equity – the level of gearing or leverage.
(b) The planned relationship between the earnings from the company's business and the costs of servicing its funding – interest cover.
(c) Dividend policy.
(d) The circumstances in and terms on which it might wish to raise additional equity – equity dilution.
(e) The amount and nature of liquid funds/undrawn facilities needed or desired.
(f) The mix of ranking of obligations:
    (i)   ordinary equity (usually subordinated to everyone including preference shareholders);
    (ii) preference share capital ('non-equity share capital');
    (iii) subordinated debt;
    (iv) senior debt.
(g) The maturity of the obligation – short, medium, long, perpetual.
(h) The effective currency mix of the obligations and their servicing (against the same for the assets or their earning power).
(i) The effective mix of floating and fixed rate or rate-capped obligations and the periods of fixings/caps.
(j) The cocktail of providers of funds/facilities and instruments by which risks are adjusted.

The policy chosen will depend on the business to be financed and its characteristics including its underlying risks, earnings potential and the ambitions of the management as regards expansion, etc. The available policies will depend, often crucially, on the existing financial profile of the company, inherited from the successes and failures of policies (or lack of policies) of the past. And the available *suppliers* of funds and risk management products will also be conditioned to some extent by the pre-existing relationships.

Clearly, the amounts and types of funding and financial risk reduction it is possible to put in place and their cost will frequently feed back into the business plan, influencing growth rates, target trading profit margins, target rates of return on investment, etc.

The perceived importance of any one element of a company's strategy varies with its circumstances. A well capitalised company with high cash earnings from a well protected market position may give little time to financial strategy or its components or to the policies dealing with individual variables appropriate to the strategy at any particular time. To such companies, financial strategy is in many ways a residual determined by the marketing and production strategies, for example. A company on the border-line of bankruptcy during a recession may find that it becomes its major preoccupation, strategies in other areas being largely subordinated to it. Both of these extremes are suboptimal: financial strategy should play its part alongside other strategies of the firm.

A suitable financial strategy contributes, sometimes crucially, to both the cash flows themselves and the level of risk associated with them. Success or failure of financial policy can be a major element in determining the value of the company – if any.

The place of banks in financial strategy

Clearly 'banks' are very likely to feature in the last item of financial policy set out above: the cocktail of providers of funds/facilities and instruments by which risks are adjusted. Also, cash is the lifeblood of any business and banks are the principal providers of the means by which it moves between the business's sources and stores of funds and its applications of them. For most companies, the crucial role of banks is that of provider of funds. Increasingly as we saw in earlier chapters, it is that of the 'arranger' of funds.

In general, non-financial corporations in most countries have preferred to fund themselves internally, with retained earnings. Indeed, according to CEPR's International Study of Corporate Finance between 1970 and 1989, in France, Japan and Germany 64.5 per cent, 71.7 per cent and 80.6 per cent respectively of net sources of finance were from retentions. In the United States it was 91.3 per cent and in the United Kingdom 98.0 per cent. Yet companies still borrowed substantial amounts, much of it from banks (bonds accounted for only 9 per cent of net new borrowing by UK companies; US: 51 per cent). In both the US and the UK, 'equity' was a drain on company funding – mainly due to mergers and acquisitions.

Banks, then, as lenders, have been crucial to the funding of the general business strategies (i.e. strategies for acquisition) of United Kingdom and United States companies. Bonds issues in France, Germany and Japan accounted for only a small part of net new borrowings (from *minus* 6 per cent (Germany) to plus 8 per cent (Japan)) and banks were crucial lenders, funding their internal investment strategies.

Why is it that companies have borrowed from banks rather than sold bonds? The answers are many:

(a) Ease of access (banks are more understanding of lesser or 'difficult' credits).
(b) A facility can more easily be structured to meet a company's needs in face to face discussion with one or a few banks in a way impossible in capital markets which generally want more standardised products.
(c) Availability in large amounts at relatively short notice and without publicity (all-important in acquisition finance).
(d) Availability on a stand-by basis (effectively an option) with medium-term commitment.
(e) Ability to be drawn when needed and repaid when not.
(f) Sometimes, cost.

Banks have also been important suppliers of non-lending but still credit risk-bearing products – swaps, guarantees, etc.

The real test of the arrangements, as noted earlier, comes when trends turn and the good times become hard. Then, the weak links break. After the turn, more companies remember and try to take into account again that:

> *Stabilisation of the economy through monetary policy works through credit crunches.* It does not work through the seamless, incremental fine-tuning that is possible only in the textbook economic models but not in the real world. Monetary restraint operates not so much by restraining everyone in an economy a little bit, inducing all of us to change our economic behaviour marginally, but by restraining some individuals, firms or institutions a great deal – by strictly limiting or even eliminating access to credit altogether for marginal borrowers. (Dr Henry Kaufman, speech to National Association of Business Economists, 1991.)

Banking relationships were often severely tested in the 'credit crunches' in the United States and United Kingdom as the 1980s became the 1990s.

Banking relationships and credit standing

By 1991, when the trends had turned and banks began to cut back their activities as capital ratios became too geared or new rules demanded they become less geared and the credit standing of some companies began to weaken, both sides found that transaction-oriented banks had a relatively shallow grasp of the realities of the company's business and a corresponding level of commitment. (Commitment, here, is used in the sense of feeling some 'moral obligation' to stick with a company over the medium or long term.)

One disaffected bank with no commitment to the company could jeopardise or cause to miscarry the plans of a company to carry on its business – or of other banks to achieve the best solution for all creditors.

Selecting the right relationships with the right cocktail of banks is important to the standing of the company. Companies will normally seek to establish a set of banking relationships including commercial and investment banks which will service their needs at reasonable cost on reasonable terms and conditions, in good times and in bad. In general, they will have a couple of leading banks, a handful of other banks they consider very important and a number of other banks making up the 'also rans', but which might include key specialists in particular focused areas. Some of the banks will bring their powerful balance sheets and ability to lend to the company; some will bring capital markets distribution abilities; some will be efficient market makers in certain instruments or competitive providers of 'over the counter' products (e.g. options, interest rate caps); some will advise on acquisitions and disposals and how to avoid being taken over; and some will contribute useful, well thought out ideas.

Companies that have lost their credit standing will find that they are yoked to a group of banks inherited from the good times. Their agreement has to be obtained on many issues and there is no question of directing banking business elsewhere. If it involves credit risk, no other bank will take it on. If it involves no credit risk, it will involve fee income and the supporting group of banks will insist on having it.

The risk to other creditors from weakly committed banks even if they have signed up to legal agreements to provide accommodation under certain terms and conditions over a certain period ('committed' facilities) is well known to the credit rating agencies.

> In assessing various sources of funding, Moody's gives significant weight to relationship-based committed borrowing facilities. In periods of company or market related stress, it is more likely that relationship lenders will move to stabilise a company's liquidity position when market and transaction-oriented lenders have fled (Moody's Special Report, January 1991).

And it goes beyond lending, of course. Companies will be involved in other forms of credit relationship with a bank – as lessees, as counterparties in swaps, as counter-indemnifiers in bonds and guarantees and letters of credit issued by the bank, and as guarantors of third party liabilities (e.g. of subsidiaries of the client), for example.

A company's credit standing is not only important to debt holders (who are the most avid readers of credit rating agency reports). It has significance for holders of non-equity share capital (preference shares) and equity (ordinary share) holders as it is a measure of their risk in this area. Not all investors are able to diversify their risk over the whole market and so be unaffected by firm specific risks. Their risk may be that the company will need a rights issue (credit standing becomes too weak) requiring share-holders to stump up more cash or face dilution of their holding. Or, it may be that the risk is loss, or partial loss, of their investment – insolvency or corporate restructuring. While the diversified investor is in theory indifferent to individual company failure, even the largest does not actually welcome loss of its investment.

A company's credit standing also has significance for suppliers and even for customers and potential customers. (Tandem Computer took this as far as shunning borrowing of any kind in its early days: 'We were a young company competing with the likes of IBM. Not taking on debt was a marketing decision because we might not get customers if we seemed financially shaky.' ('Has the debt binge gone too far?' K Bullen, *Fortune*, April 1988))

To understand a client company as a credit risk and to understand it as a customer – that is, what products the company might be sold and how they should be sold to it – takes the time of knowledgeable, senior officers of a bank.

The good banking relationship

Compared with other providers of corporate funding, banks have a comparative advantage in gathering information about and in monitoring corporate borrowers. This comes from their continuing business with the company (sometimes including current account operation) and their ability to talk to management as part of the client relationship. Banks are thus in a position to reduce the costs (risks) associated with the informational disadvantages of other stakeholders in a firm relative to its management.

The essence of good banking relationships for a company, then, is to exploit the favoured position of banks to the mutual benefit of both themselves and the banks.

It is not possible for a company to have a personal, one-to-one relationship with very many banks. It takes too much corporate management time. To have this kind of relationship with a weak bank, for one reason or another unable or unwilling to respond to corporate needs as it might, is a waste of valuable opportunity for a company. Equally, the cost to the banks of the relationship is high and the advantage will be lost if it is spread over too small a volume of business.

Accordingly, a company needs a small number of 'relationship' banks from which it purchases differentiated or strongly differentiated products. A large company will have more such banks, a smaller one, fewer (see Chapter 6). A company, particularly a large one with operations (or subsidiary operations) internationally, will also have an 'outer circle' of banks from which it purchases non-differentiated or weakly differentiated products in competition with the 'relationship' banks. It may also purchase from the outer circle some strongly differentiated products which, while important to some part of the business (e.g. an overseas subsidiary in a difficult territory) are not of major importance to the group as a whole.

The company will expect its relationship banks to be responsive to its needs and responsible in their attitudes to the company. The relationship banks will expect to be kept informed in general terms about the company's plans and progress and likely future needs of products they may be able to deliver. They expect to be asked to quote for a reasonable proportion of the company's business for which they have indicated ability and appetite.

The relationship bank will expect to know the financial manager and some of the general managers of the company and to have learned to respect their abilities and understanding of the business they run and its circumstances. The company will expect the banks to confine the use of any 'inside' information given to them as relationship banks to the purpose for which it was intended and not to disseminate it further – even to other departments of the bank (with the universal exception of the credit department).

Finally, the market has a long memory for past failures but a short one for past successes. Any business relationship will be entirely dependent on the parties' evaluation of its future. For the company: will the bank offer the services it seeks – competitively, congenially, quickly and in adequate quantity? For the bank: will the customer offer, in the long run, a return commensurate with the risk and in a volume and across a sufficient range of products for the bank to recover its servicing costs (including required profit)? Past service may feed nostalgia but it is not relevant to the future except as it influences expectations about that future.

6 Developing banking relationships: the corporate viewpoint

In this chapter we first consider the differences between theory and practice in the area of corporate banking relations, and, in the light of these, then go on to discuss the criteria that the corporate treasurer might use in selecting and developing relationships with the company's bankers.

Theory and practice

As pointed out earlier, no business can operate without at least one bank; indeed, for businesses of any size it is sensible to use more than one. This is not just to use competition as a mechanism for keeping them all on their toes, though that can be a helpful side-effect. While many banks can justifiably claim to offer a full range of services, no single bank is best at everything. For the treasurer, the decision as to how many banks to use is a question of balance. The treasurer needs to ensure that there is at least one bank which is thoroughly competent in each of the business areas in which the company requires service but, at the same time, the limited amounts of worthwhile business the company has to offer must not be spread so thinly that the company ceases to be of importance to any of the bankers. This would be inimical to the building of any substantial relationship. Why does this matter?

From the banks' standpoint, customer relationships are primarily a marketing tool. A good relationship will often provide a regular flow of business and always offer the prospect of new business opportunities. Since this leaves the diligent account officer looking uncomfortably like a second-hand car salesperson, other reasons are often given by banks for seeking to establish relationships. A valid one is that working with a customer over an extended timescale enables the bank to build up its knowledge base of the customer's business and, as a result, makes it better able to develop products that will be relevant and helpful. The value of this should not be underestimated.

However, an argument which is much less readily sustainable, but is never the less often heard, is that for a bank to trade with a relationship customer is less risky than undertaking *ad hoc* business. The hard truth is that, regardless of the existence or otherwise of an ongoing relationship, the bank which lends without having carried out adequate credit control checks has only itself to blame in the event of subsequent difficulty. Indeed, the moral pressure on a bank to provide additional support if things do start to go wrong for the customer will clearly be greater where there has been a long term relationship; thus it can equally be argued that relationship business puts the banks at greater, rather than less, risk. Several US and British banks have had first hand experience of the problems of 'work-out' or 'bail-out' situations.

This is the reverse side of the argument most often put forward as to why long term banking relationships are important for companies. The old adage defines a banker as someone who will always lend you an umbrella provided that it is not raining; corporate treasurers must always be mindful of the fact that it could rain for their company. No matter how strong the business, it can always be undermined by such events as technological change, economic downturn, social prejudice or fashion fancy. In such a situation it is almost certain that the company will want to borrow additional funds and it will be the treasurer's task to persuade the bankers that it is appropriate for them to lend. The theory is that this will be easier if there is an established relationship.

Whether or not this will prove to be true in practice will depend on three major factors:

(a) How serious is the company's position? Is there a reasonable expectation that additional finance will enable it to survive and generate sufficient cash flow to repay both the new and old debt, or will the bank just find itself sucked in deeper and deeper as it is forced to roll-up interest charges into an ever compounding mountain of debt? No matter how strong the relationship, the bank will have to take a realistic view of its customer's prospects. There is no point in shooting a second arrow after the first if everything points only to a further loss.

(b) What is the bank's current position? There can be something of a paradox here. One might think that the stronger and more liquid its position at the time, the more ready it would be to assume the risk of providing further support. The reality could be quite different and depend on the state of the bank's balance sheet. The alternative to further support for the customer will normally involve receivership for the company and a provision, if not a write-off, for the bank. If you owe the bank £1000 and cannot repay then you have a problem; but if you owe the bank £1 000 000 and cannot repay then it is the bank that has the problem.

(c) What is the nature of the relationship? Since there is little the treasurer can do about the first two issues, it is this that must be addressed if he or she is seriously concerned about building relationships that the company can depend on in adversity.

One has to begin with a recognition that, in the face of the risk inherent in any loan, the temptation for any lending officer is to be defensive; such an approach can manifest itself in either or both of two ways. The first is that of the pawnbroker who is willing to lend only up to a fixed proportion of an estimate of the realisable value of the asset that the borrower pledges as security for the debt. This approach is all too common among bankers handling relatively small companies. The position is not helped by the fact that the lending decision is often taken remotely on the basis of a piece of paper rather than by the appraisal of the individual and the project.

The pawnbroker approach is likely to be less relevant in the case of major companies especially when the issue is not one of further support to a company that is for any reason ailing. Here, defensiveness is more likely to take the second form, that of safety in numbers: 'I can't be blamed if I do what everyone else does.' For the treasurer of a large company then, having one or two banks on which he or she can rely can be of particular importance since others are likely to be willing to follow their lead.

How then does one set about establishing a relationship which, in difficult though not impossible circumstances, can reasonably be expected to withstand these pressures. Undoubtedly the first step is to be sure that the bank in question does not see itself as a pawnbroker; that it is looking at the total ongoing business of the company as the security for its loan rather than at the realisable value of the relevant assets. Notice that it is the attitude of the bank as a whole that matters, not just that of an individual or group of individuals within the bank. Probing each bank's policy in this area must therefore be a key issue for any company when it reviews its banking relationships. Of course, a bank can change its policy in this or any other connection; but its staff are more likely to change and, more important, in the final analysis it will be the policy of the bank rather than the opinion of an individual that matters.

This is not to say that account officers are unimportant in a relationship. Chemistry between individuals can have very real effects and it is important that the individuals representing the two parties to the relationship get on well together. Further, depending on how the organisation of the bank is structured, the diligence and technical competence of the account officer may be a controlling factor in determining whether or not the company enjoys the full benefit of the services that the bank is capable of delivering. None of this, however, is relevant to the fundamental issue of whether or not support would be forthcoming in adverse circumstances. Clearly it would be important that the account officer argued the company's case within the bank, and was of sufficient standing to guarantee a hearing; but this would hardly be likely if the account officer knew that his or her ideas ran contrary to the bank's policy.

The building blocks of the relationship

Given that these various problems can be overcome, what arguments are available to persuade the bank to offer the needed support? Here one comes back to the concept that the security for any loan to a company is the totality of its ongoing business. It follows that the bank must be given an opportunity of evaluating the strength of that business. To this end it needs to evaluate not only the company's finances but also the quality of its management, its technology and its markets. It will be too late to expect such an approach once the company has run into trouble; the assessment must be made in advance and be updated regularly.

From the corporate standpoint then, the first rule on building banking relationships is that it is best done in the good times when the business is healthy and its prospects are bright. Note though that, for the brave banker, the reverse can be true; help provided in a time of difficulty is likely to be appreciated and remembered long after more normal transactions are forgotten.

Banks vary in their willingness to build a proper understanding of the nature of their customer's business and, in fairness, it has to be recognised that the effort involved in doing so may not be proportionate to the advantage to be gained. Treasurers should accordingly encourage and seek to exploit such interest as the chosen bank may show. Among the steps that might be taken are:

(a) The provision of annual reports and accounts and of periodic published results.
(b) The provision of other textual information describing the products, manufacturing facilities and other aspects of the business.
(c) Talking to executives of the bank about the business and its prospects, but in general terms without disclosing price-sensitive information.
(d) Facilitating visits to company sites by banks' representatives.
(e) Arranging for senior officials of the bank to meet members of the company's board.

Some amplification of this last point may be helpful.

The advantage of introducing an element of discipline into such meetings must be obvious. These meetings should have a purpose. Sometimes they are treated as no more than an opportunity for a senior visiting banker to meet the most senior available corporate officer who can be made available and the meeting will as a result consist only of pleasantries. The real object of the exercise should only be to allow the banker to increase his/her understanding of the company's business and, perhaps more important, to assess the quality of its senior management. The participants are inevitably busy people and it is important to both that they should exploit the opportunity afforded by the time they have made available. That said, the treasurer does have a responsibility to protect the senior oficer from unnecessary visits. As far as possible the participants in meetings of this type should be matched by seniority, but this must be qualified to reflect the relative sizes of the bank and the company. Similarly, senior executives should only be asked to make time available for banks with which the company has an established relationship or with which there is a specific intention to form such a relationship.

Building a relationship will, of course, involve contact at many different levels and, while those made at the most senior are likely to prove the most important at times of crisis, the relationship needs to be built on a firm foundation of satisfactory contact on a day-to-day basis at all levels. Corporate treasurers will inevitably be the focus of contact with each bank and should ensure that they have good working relationships at a number of levels, both above and beneath their own, within those banks that they deem to be of sufficient importance to the company to justify the time and effort involved. Dependent on how the bank is organised, corporate treasurers may well use their designated account officer as the main interface, but they need to be sure that, where the issue justifies it, they can readily go up the line within the bank to ensure that the problem is receiving proper attention.

Treasurers should also ensure that their staff have reasonable opportunities to meet and get to know the members of staff of the banks with whom they themselves have to deal. Such contact need not be wholly social, though luncheons and social events have their place where the relationships are strong. Relationships of this kind are, of course, built for a different purpose from that which has been considered up to this point. They are concerned essentially with the smooth running of financial operations rather than with bank support in times of difficulty. As such, they are at least equally important, if only because the need for them is so very much more certain. For example, where dealing staff are concerned, the fact that the corporate staff are known personally to the dealers in the banks with whom they trade achieves an additional degree of security, provided that it is recognised that it could open the door to collusion.

Here then, we have the two main considerations of which a company will take account in deciding what sorts of relationships it wishes to build, and with which banks. First, it must decide which bank will be most likely to provide support in times of difficulty and, second, it must decide which bank will be best able to provide the types of service it expects to require. The degree of importance that the company attaches to each will vary, probably dependent on its state of health. However, in all normal circumstances, it should not be impossible to satisfy both criteria.

Choosing relationship banks

Against this background, as an integral element of its financial strategy, every company has to choose one or more banks with which to do business; how many should it have? There is no short answer to this question. 'As few as possible' would mean only one, since the major banks would certainly claim that they can provide any service that a company requires even though they might have mixed feelings about being sole banker to the very largest companies. Certainly, if the company is of any size and is serious about its treasury activities, it will wish to be in a position to ensure that its banks have to compete for its business; the use of a single bank might facilitate the building of a very strong relationship, but it would preclude competition. Further it would leave the company in a very exposed position with no fall-back relationship to which to turn in the event that its bank, for whatever reason, saw fit to withdraw its support. Indeed, however good the relationship and however well behaved the bank, the company would be exposed to the threat of withdrawal in any negotiation between them.

Nor is the argument that any one bank can provide all the services that a company requires wholly valid. While the statement is probably true for a number of the very largest banks, this is not to say that all banks are equally good at all aspects of banking business. In regard to the straightforward elements of domestic banking such as running cheque accounts, the standard is very high and there will be little to choose between the services offered by the major commercial banks; there may be a price differential from time to time but this will be a matter for negotiation. Generally speaking, the corporate treasurer can take it for granted that the 'back office' services will be of a very high standard.

However, in the international field and in specialist areas of banking it is possible to distinguish between the qualities of service offered by different banks. Obviously, banks that have a large international branch network will be able to offer better value-dating of transfers than those that are dependent on reciprocal arrangements. Here the company's choice of banks may be determined by the need for relationship banking in a number of different countries. Similarly there are banks that specialise in financing trade with specific third world territories; where this service is of sufficient value to a company, it may feel justified in building a broad relationship with the bank concerned in order to enjoy the benefit of this specialist service.

More likely to be a sensitive area for the company is the question of fundraising. Every company will want to be sure that its bank is willing and, more important, has the strength to support at least its seasonal funding needs. Beyond this, the larger companies will expect their commercial bankers to be willing to take a substantial position in the funding of their medium term requirements. What constitutes a substantial position will depend largely on the size of the company. All banks have limits for the total exposure they are prepared to accept with any single customer; legal lending limits in the case of US banks. Accordingly, while smaller companies can look to their banks to fund all of their medium term requirements, larger companies must normally expect to borrow from a number of different banks, usually on a syndicated basis.

It does not follow from this that a company would necessarily expect all of its major relationship commercial banks to be able to lead its syndicated medium term borrowing operations; it may even prefer to turn to its investment bank for this service. However, in choosing its relationship bankers it will wish to ensure that at least one of them enjoys the market status that will enable it to do so; indeed, preferably more than one since an element of competition is likely to prove advantageous for the company.

This begs the question as to the terms on which a company should seek to borrow in the medium term bank market. Should it, on the one hand, use its full financial muscle in order to drive the hardest bargain possible regardless of any longer term implications? Such an approach is likely to draw a relatively weak group of banks into the syndicate, the commitment of which may be less reliable than is desirable; nor are such banks likely to be supportive should the company encounter problems during the life of the loan. Should the company then, on the other hand, accept whatever terms its trusted relationship bank offers?

The best approach lies somewhere between these two extremes, with the corporate treasurer involving the banks in some form of controlled competition. To do this will require a close knowledge of the market; the treasurer will need to know how the various banks operate and at what levels recent transactions have been carried out. Working, as is inevitably the case, at one stage removed from the market, it is difficult for any corporate treasurer to have the necessary insight; on major syndicated borrowing operations it may well be sensible to seek advice. Perhaps the obvious source for such advice is an investment bank; however, to be of real value, it is essential that the advice be genuinely independent and appropriately rewarded. Accordingly, it will be better to obtain it from a party that has no other interest in the transaction.

It is, of course, to its investment bank, rather than to a commercial bank, that the company will expect to turn for major capital transactions such as equity and loan stock issues. Here again, there are banks that would claim to be able to fulfil both functions but it is unrealistic to suggest that a company of any size should operate without an investment bank. How then should a company set about structuring its banking relationships?

Structuring banking relationships

In any given territory, the company should have at least one house bank. 'House bank' is a term commonly used in Continental Europe to indicate the lead bank in the company's day-to-day banking operations as well as the first port of call for finance. The more usual US and UK term is 'lead bank' which does not imply the same level of 'working together'. Increasingly, the largest companies refer to their banking relationships in terms of a 'core' group supported by a secondary, probably more specialised, group. The likelihood is that history will dictate which bank this is and no company should change without very good reason. It is unlikely that quality of service would justify a change; competition on banks' charges might be a consideration, especially in a company such as a retail organisation which has a large number of cash transactions. In all normal circumstances, however, any problems that arise in the course of routine domestic banking should be capable of resolution without the upheaval and expense that a change of house bank would inevitably involve.

In recent times, we have seen one or two companies publicly change long standing domestic banking relationships on the ground that their banker has provided financial support to a predator company in a takeover situation. Such transactions can place a bank in a difficult position, especially where it has relationships with both the predator and target companies. One course would be to decide which side was most likely to win, support it, and accept the risk of loss of the other account. However, in the longer term, it may be better to behave in a wholly open manner to both parties, but not provide direct support to either. In any event, careful consideration will have to be given as to the bank's legal position and, in particular, to any confidential information it holds on either party.

The services that the house bank can be expected to provide are primarily those related to the administration of current accounts. Nowadays, this will be expected to involve electronic banking, including computer to computer transfers of data. It is these types of arrangement that tend to lock companies into their house banks, though in reality the other issues discussed earlier in the chapter are of much greater, if less readily quantifiable, significance.

In association with the current account, the house bank will also provide short term credit facilities. In the UK these are called 'overdraft' facilities. Companies tend to place greater value on these than is properly justified. While an overdraft is generally subject to annual review, it can none the less be called by the bank at any time without prior warning of any kind. As a form of finance it is accordingly unreliable and, more important, it can often be the weak link in a company's financing structure; if called, not only must the debt be repaid on the same day, but the very calling will usually, albeit technically, constitute a default under the cross-default clauses in the company's other loan agreements. While the banks will undoubtedly argue that they would never call in a debt without good reason, the exposure involved in the use of a standard overdraft is such that the corporate treasurer should keep the position under constant review. Following the BIS guidelines on cost of capital, banks everywhere are now unwilling to set aside finance in case it is needed unless the company is prepared to pay a fee. Again however, the question of a fee is subject to competitive pressures.

That said, good liquidity management almost demands a limited use of such facilities since, without doing so, it is virtually impossible to avoid having regular uninvested cash surpluses. Beyond this, an overdraft is likely to be a relatively expensive means of borrowing for any but the shortest time periods. It is true that, from time to time, government activity in the money market can offer large companies opportunities to use their overdraft facilities for arbitrage purposes, borrowing on overdraft and depositing at a turn back in the market from which the banks have themselves had to find the funds to lend. Such activity will readily be seen by the banks and will do nothing for the longer term relationships. Banks recognise that companies are technically fully entitled to exploit such opportunities, but overdraft facilities are not provided for this purpose.

In addition to domestic payments, the house banks will also be used for making international payments. However, this need not imply that the house bank should enjoy all, or even most, of the company's foreign exchange business. This is one area of banking business which is generally recognised to be wholly open to competition. As part of an ongoing relationship, one would expect the house banks to be given a fair share of opportunities to bid for deals but beyond this it is not necessary to go. Banks do have expertise and other strengths in specific currencies which the corporate treasurer should seek to exploit. Standard arrangements should be put in place with the bank that is responsible for making the company's international payments, so that currency bought anywhere in the market can be transferred into appropriate clearing accounts for use.

Large international banks, and some not so large, often use foreign exchange trading as a route to the establishment of a broader banking relationship. Banks that are house banks in other territories will also seek to exploit their relationships in order to obtain a foothold with the treasury department of the holding company. There is no justification for objecting to this, within reason. Such secondary relationships can be useful in building up awareness of the company in the market and ease subsequent syndication problems. Furthermore, this is often a way for a

Table 6.1 The banking structure of a company

	Major company	Large company
House banks – domestic	1–3	1
House banks – international per territory	1	1
Secondary banks – in home country	8	5
Investment banks – home country	2	1
Investments banks – per relevant territory	1	1

secondary bank to break into the 'core' group. However, it is essential to contain the number of secondary banking relationships since failure to do so can readily lead to a situation in which the company is spreading its business so thinly that no bank is going to feel that the attendant relationship is of any significance to it.

The banking structure for a company might then be established along the lines of Table 6.1.

These are only guidelines and suggestions; much will depend on circumstance. It is likely that there will be considerable overlap between categories with individual banks fulfilling more than one role. Even so it will readily be seen that a major international company could easily find itself having relationships with 50 or more banks of which up to 10 might constitute the 'core' group.

7 The place of corporate relationships in bank strategy

As we saw in earlier chapters it is becoming difficult to divide banks into neat categories. We may talk of commercial and investment banks – along with local variations – but they have functions in common and much overlap. Some of the larger banks have become global in every sense; both geographical and in their range of activities. Others have reinvented themselves.

With this as background together with the knowledge that banking is in ferment, we shall in this chapter examine the thinking behind banking strategy in the area of relationships.

Relationship and transaction banking

Relationship banking implies a personal ease, ideally attaching to the whole of both sides; a mutual confidence in competence and integrity; and mutual loyalty. In practical terms, the bank must make enough profit overall not to insist on large profits on each service; the company must receive value to justify its cost.

Loyalty is a two way process, but the need for it tends to come at different times. In good times some companies discount the value of relationships; then banks need loyalty, and must justify it. In recession or times of tight money, or when they are in trouble, clients need the banks' loyalty; they may be shocked if their lack of it is reciprocated.

Transaction banking, in its purest form, is any service, or closely linked group of services, that a bank performs for a fee. The client's decision to work with a particular bank is based solely on the bank's bid or expected performance with no link to any relationship, or future business. Loan syndications, swaps, bond underwriting, mergers and acquisitions, and private placement are examples.

A transaction bank puts more weight on specific pieces of business than on a relationship. A transaction client allocates each transaction separately. Transaction banking has been graphically described as 'hit and run' banking.

Relationship banker

A relationship banker's progress is judged on the bank's profits from his or her group of clients, not from any product. The relationship banker must sell the bank's products, but also judge which are appropriate in each case, and build up clients' confidence in his or her advice, sometimes even being paid partly for the advice rather than the product. Relationship bankers must ensure that their clients get the best possible product, so that sometimes they will advise a client to use another bank. If they have to do this often, there is something wrong with their bank's range of products, or with their internal communications. Nevertheless, to do this may add credibility to later advice to use a product for which their own bank is not well known.

Product banker

The product banker's job is to sell a product. Product bankers will pay some attention to the client's needs, but to enable them to sell more products, not in the client's wider interest. They may use hard sell techniques, unconcerned that these will damage the overall interests of the bank. Where the product involves taking positions, the product banker will cut price to cover an open position, and give this opportunity to the first comer rather than select among the bank's best clients.

Particularly where the product involves a major fee, such as M&A, the pressure to get the deal done and earn the fee may override the client's interest, even where the bank has a fiduciary duty to give objective advice.

Commercial = relationship; investment = transaction?

Commercial banks incline towards relationship banking partly because their products, lending in particular, tend to be continuing rather than one-off. This reduces the prospect that a single mistake will wreck the whole relationship. Take money transmission, for instance, or global custody. Clients expect the quality of these services to be good, and for some companies this is the most

important service a bank can offer. But even the best banks make
some mistakes; moreover, changing banks is a long and costly affair,
often for no improvement. Continuing failure to deliver a quality
product damages the relationship; but the bank will probably have
time to correct individual mistakes or weaknesses.

To some extent the reverse is true with investment banking
products. The product range is often relatively narrow: equity
underwriting; M&A. Each client uses each product relatively
infrequently, so that even where there is a relationship, the profits
come from a few big deals rather than a stream of business. Each
deal is critical for the client, so that a failure, sometimes for reasons
outside the bank's control, may undermine confidence and wreck
the relationship; or in M&A, the bank may have clients on both
sides and be unable to act for either. Of course there are other
aspects: the size of the deals makes keeping the relationship more
important to the bank; successful completion gets attention at the
highest levels in the company and builds loyalty; and at least some
companies do a steady stream of equity or debt issues, or
acquisitions, so that they almost amount to annuity business.

What type of strength?

Against these general descriptions, each bank needs to decide what
type, if any, of relationship it wants to develop. This will depend on
the general type of bank it is, and its own particular strength. A bank
cannot decide its relationship strategy unless it knows what type of
bank it wants to be, and its strength. Changes in the strategy can be
hard on relationships, as bankers find themselves having to switch
tack, and often annoying their clients in the process.

Capital structure and pricing objectives

Banks must also decide the type of capital structure and return they
want. The type of bank and product often set the parameters which
in turn affect relationships. Banks have two categories of earnings:
annuity earnings and transaction earnings. Annuity earnings arise
from continuous service of some sort: lending, money trans-
missions, deposits, etc. Transaction earnings arise from the fees on
single transactions, or unconnected series of transactions.
Traditionally, commercial banks were more likely to have annuity
products, investment banks transaction products. Annuity earnings,
continuous and reliable, are often lower, especially in competitive
conditions. They also tend to be more capital intensive in both

financial and physical capital. Transactions tend to be less capital intensive, more cost intensive; M&A for instance needs little capital, but high personnel costs.

Capital intensity carries high fixed costs, so reliable earnings are important to service them. However, the decline in the margins available meant that while steady, annuity earnings were insufficient. Some commercial banks therefore tried to generate transaction fees; as annuity earnings shrank, fees replaced rather than supplemented them.

Investment banks were historically more transaction- and fee-oriented, although many also had trading operations, which again are capital intensive. While some of these relied for profits on taking big positions in the various markets, others relied on a small turn from a high volume of client trades. And while the underwriting of corporate bonds and shares might be transaction banking, distribution of the underwritten paper required relationships.

It was never true, therefore, that all commercial banks were solely relationship-oriented, and all investment banks transaction-oriented. For example, British merchant banks were more relationship conscious than the big commercial banks. Nevertheless, the business each type of bank did tended to push it towards either relationship or transaction banking. Few banks went all the way in either direction; even before competition cut margins on annuity earnings, relationship banks wanted a share of the transaction jam; transaction banks still try to establish a relationship claim on future transactions.

Nevertheless, the overlap between the two has become greater. More commercial banks try to arrange or underwrite loans for fees, keeping less of the loan for themselves to provide annuity earnings. They also compete with investment banks for other fee business, from arranging transactions such as syndications, through various types of bond underwriting, to private placements, structured financings, M&A and so on. Swaps and other derivatives are neither fish nor fowl, so that all types of banks compete for them. Commercial banks have also been keen in recent years to sell down debt assisting the process of debt handling and securitisation.

Fitting the strategy to strengths and client needs

Each bank therefore needs a strategy that fits its marketing strengths, but also meets other criteria, which are described at greater length in Chapter 8. These include risk management strengths, the risk profile, the pricing criteria, and the client's desires (which may reflect a misunderstanding of the bank's strengths).

Conflict between strategy and client's desires can leave the bank with a difficult decision: whether to accept the client's view and waive its strategy for that client; or risk upsetting the client; or close the relationship because it does not fit in with the strategy.

The answer depends partly on whether the bank thinks it can change the client's mind, partly on the value of the relationship. But mainly it depends on the thrust of the bank's strategy. Is it adding a few bells and whistles to its product range? Or an important business to its portfolio? Or changing its classification altogether? The balance between keeping the client happy and fulfilling the strategy will be different in each case.

Linkage

Linkage ties a service or a risk to the promise of specific business. This may seem the essence of relationship banking; but by tying one transaction to another, rather than to overall profitability, it is more like its negation. There is often no check that the linked transactions taken together are profitable. The linkage may tempt the bank to take a submarginal credit risk, disproportionate to any return. Or it may be one sided, and may not influence the earnings. Or it can blur the image of the bank as pricing to combine profit with value for money. The true cost then may not be the loss on the particular transaction, but the ability to get a fair price from other clients with no linkage.

The strategy decision as to what businesses a bank stays in, and why, affects the ability to link. For instance, operating services in overseas branches may no longer be profitable, nor fit the strategy. But many clients use them, and do other business with the bank. Can the bank close down the service without losing other business? Banks often find that clients recognise the anomaly; or are willing to pay more. Or clients who hardly seem to use it may be deeply upset to find it withdrawn.

These reactions then have to be set against the reasons for withdrawing. For some, the client reaction may decide the bank to keep it at a higher price. For others the question may be 'how do we get out with least damage to relationships?' rather than 'do we get out?'

The more difficult decision covers what might be called the core services, particularly lending. A main line commercial bank can hardly step out of the lending business overnight, even if it wants to. It also has to decide whether its aim is to change the character of the bank permanently, or merely to shift with the market cycle. Even if it initially thinks the change is permanent, it may find developments make it less so.

Or it may lose skills, particularly credit skills, which it will later need. Much of investment banking involves credit risk and judgement even if in a different form from straightforward lending; so do products such as swaps and foreign exchange. And if the bank does have to move back towards lending, its loss of credit skills can be very expensive. It therefore needs a strategy on credit which must fit with all other aspects of the strategy.

Problems caused by the bank withdrawing from some products or services

There are connections between products that only become obvious when you try to abolish one. Short term lending, for years a valued product, in the late 1970s and 1980s became less profitable and less important; banks withdrew to varying extents. Their treasuries, however, needed assets on which to earn funding margins and started buying floating rate notes (FRNs), commercial paper or even bank loans from the same borrowers to whom the bank refused to lend direct, in the money markets. At least one general manager and his credit officer turned down a loan to a borrower in the morning at an eighth *over* LIBOR (London Inter-Bank Offered Rate), to find that the sterling treasurer was delighted to have brought paper for the same issuer at an eighth *below* LIBOR.

These and similar experiences caused some banks to review their approach to short term lending; they decided in many cases to lend direct rather than to do so indirectly at lower spreads. It made for better credit control, and also helped relationships with companies that liked the offer of short term credit, even on a less committed basis than traditional lines. It also gave the bank a reason to talk to clients' treasury people, a prime element in maintaining relationships. These were collateral benefits; the main one was to give the treasury an asset base.

Short term money market lending helps to manage the balance sheet and liquidity. A bank can refuse to lend, or raise its price, as it suits the book. An alternative is to sell a loan and remove it from the books for capital and funding purposes. This has both advantages and disadvantages for the client: cheaper or larger loans against loss of control over who its lender is. The point here, however, is not the merits or demerits of loan sales and money market lending; it is rather the possible clash between what the client wants and the bank's strategy.

Where these clashes arise, a relationship bank has to juggle with the strategy and the client's wish/need. It is in business to meet its clients' needs. However, a high quality service costs far more than any one or two clients can meet; to provide it for only a few may be impractical. It is often loss of profitability that causes the bank to review its strategy in the first place. And it may not be merely a question of cost, but of credit standards, how to train staff or even the type of staff to hire; all these are part of the strategy, or of the tools needed to implement it.

Sometimes the client refuses to recognise the change in the banks' strategy. It is one thing to lend on unfavourable terms to a client who offers profitable investment banking; it is quite another for one who ignores your investment banking credentials. Equally with loan sales, it is one thing to give up liquidity and balance sheet flexibility, if the client pays a premium price; quite another if the client expects pricing that is predicated on the liquidity it is withholding.

These clients fail to recognise that many commercial banks are no longer automatic providers of large loans, but much more arrangers of them. To make and keep the whole loan has major implications in terms of capital, liquidity and credit control. It also removes from the bank a source of good product to sell. The potential buyers may be important clients too; moreover the need to build a distribution network requires the bank to have good product to sell; only thus can it be sure of distributing a wide range of product.

Adapting to changes in markets

A complicating factor is the rapid change in the markets, and in the attraction of various products. Profitable new products soon attract such competition that they become commodity products with (sub)commodity pricing. Often the low prices later drive out the weaker competitors, to leave a sound but unexceptional level of profits for those who hang on. Thus a true strategy has to look at more than just the present range of products; it has to look at the way in which profits rise and sink in different areas, and how the bank adapts to these changes within the strategy.

For the need to change products rapidly strains a bank. It is one factor pushing banks back from an emphasis on transaction banking towards relationship banking. If you do not know how long a product will remain in favour, it is dangerous to build a strategy around it. It is more sensible to build a relationship that you can adapt to meet changing requirements. You may not always be the top bank in the precise product your client requires today, but you are competent in that and in a range of products it may need. You are also flexible and can develop new products to meet new needs, or learn the techniques when other banks innovate. In other words you can give your client what he needs when he needs it, rather than selling him the product that suits your needs, but may not suit its.

Strategy affects, and reflects, more than just relationships

These strategic decisions are more than just how to handle relationships. They affect the bank's internal organisation, the way it handles, remunerates, trains and even recruits its staff, the qualities it seeks in staff, the capital structure required, the quality of profits and other factors. The factors in turn help shape the strategy.

The qualities needed to understand and sell a particular product are not the same as those needed to establish and maintain a relationship; indeed, part of a relationship officer's job may be to prevent unwise selling of some products.

The more old fashioned account officer handled a relatively narrow product range, and could be skilled in most aspects of it. This is no longer possible. Banks need product specialists as well as relationship officers, and the overt salesperson. Product specialists advise the client on which product meets its needs, even if it is a product in which their bank is weak. Against this, they are clearly still salespeople. No matter how much the client loves them, the contribution to the bottom line carries most weight.

The balance between the product salesperson and the relationship adviser is difficult and can lead to internal conflict. Sometimes the adviser is reluctant to push a particular product; at other times he or she may feel the client is not getting the right treatment from the product specialist. Again, unless the bank knows how profitable each product is, and keeps the information up to date, the adviser has no way of giving the right priority to products; nor management of allocating costs, revenue and remuneration between individuals, products or departments. This in turn may mean a change in internal accounting, since overall profit figures are no longer enough.

The high rate of change, in product and in margin, complicates relationship management. Banks enter a new product with great enthusiasm, and there is considerable pressure to sell it hard. Then as competition cuts margins the bank has to decide whether to press for volume to absorb the overhead, raise its prices, go for upmarket sophisticated versions or to get out. Very often it does these things one after another, while the poor salesman tears his hair out. Perhaps the worst case is where the bank goes for volume, fails to get it and gets out of the product altogether.

Against that background, banks must decide strategy, and choose tactics consistent with it. The strategy contains several parts: the overall type of bank to be, and the type of products to offer; and the level at which to compete – on price, on efficiency, on sophistication, on quality of service, on geographic spread of service, on innovation, on imagination, or on what combination of these and others. The strategy must include a management style and internal organisation that fits with these intents, and it must deal with the inherent conflicts that will arise between its different aspects.

Forms of organisation

A relationship bank must organise and staff itself so that it has the right type of relationship managers, and they have quality products to sell. It must provide succession for them; only senior and experienced people can command the necessary confidence, so that there may be no means of training within a hierarchy. Replacements must then come from people who have developed a breadth of knowledge in different product departments, and perhaps in administrative or managerial posts for a while.

This may fit the need for flexibility as products change; a transaction bank may put so much weight on one product range that a major decline in it leaves many good people with no useful function. The resulting redundancies are expensive and damaging to morale. A relationship bank can concentrate more on what its clients currently want than on any declining products with minimal redundancies.

Moving people among departments can help generate the co-operative spirit essential to relationship management; if badly done, however, it can weaken consistency and understanding of the product. To avoid this, banks may combine a backbone of product specialists who have no desire to be anything else, with star performers, who probably earn more than the departmental managers, but learn from them and move up. The specialist job can still be satisfying, but it requires management at all levels to recognise its importance.

The best relationship bank can pull together teams of people, and combinations of products, to meet each client need as it arises. This requires a spirit that looks beyond the narrow interests of a particular product or group to the interest of the bank, and client, as a whole. This depends on more than just moving people around departments. It certainly helps, however, if people can see several points of view, and if the relationship manager has an insider's idea as to what major products can be adapted to do, and what are practical forms of interdepartmental or product co-operation.

Conversely, a transaction bank still has to get the product in front of the client. It may organise so that each department markets its own product, but may find that clients are besieged by callers from many products, so that they need somebody responsible for the overall relationship. This person may at first act more as a traffic cop than a true relationship manager, but a high calibre manager will soon develop beyond that. Still, the problem of balance between product salespeople and relationship managers is always going to be difficult. It will be hardest where product salespeople see themselves as competing with each other and with the relationship manager, and especially if they see their reward as depending on doing their fellow staff member down. This can be made worse or better by remuneration systems, internal communications, rotation among jobs and so on. Whatever the details, the framework within which they operate comes from management, and comes back in a different form to the question of what type of bank management you want.

A bank that cannot convince its own people it cares about them, can hardly expect them to convince clients it cares about them. Conversely, a transaction bank needs the sales aggression to sell products to people who have no inherent bias towards buying from it.

There are questions of integrity involved, too. More banks say they put the client first than actually do so; nevertheless, relationship banks put a premium on the client's needs out of self-interest. To sell a relationship client an unsound product may be more expensive than it is worth. A transaction bank has less constraint.

This indeed is one of the problems of combining commercial and investment banking backgrounds. It is not just a question of bureaucratic controls against fast moving wheeling and dealing; it is also the extent to which the commercial banker is trained to see client service as the centre of an ethical as well as profit culture. Investment banks may not be inherently less ethical than commercial banks. Their ethical standards are certainly based on different criteria, which many commercial bankers find distasteful.

What must each side give to a relationship?

What then must a bank bring to a relationship, to turn strategy into fact? And what must a company bring, to get full value in good times and bad?

Product compatibility

To build a sound relationship strategy a bank must among other things target clients that need its product range, whether specialist or general. For instance, there is little point in soliciting loans from companies that have surplus cash and no need to borrow. Or trying to sell sophisticated tax techniques to clients firmly opposed to their use.

A client must recognise the strength of its bank, and play to those. It is wrong to break off the whole relationship because a bank either does not wish to do, or does poorly, things that it never claimed to do well. Take the question of lending, for instance. If a company wants a bank that will stand by it in difficult times, does this mean the bank must lend in whatever form the client wants and match market rates? Or does it make more sense from both points of view for the bank to say: 'If you really need us we are there, but commodity lending at market spreads is not attractive to us, and has no particular value to you.' And for the client to accept this?

Personal chemistry

Clients should not give business because 'Joe is such a nice guy;' or plays such a good game of golf. On the other hand, a bank can have a major impact on a company's future, sometimes even its survival, while to provide top quality service it needs access to sensitive information. Therefore the client must at least trust its integrity and respect its competence. Respect need not equal liking, but it often leads to it. Visits to the golf course, opera or theatre can build on the initial ease which makes the business go more smoothly. The respect and trust are the critical points, with liking and entertainment the icing on the cake.

The respect must cut both ways, most of all in lending. A lender that does not trust or respect the borrower is unlikely to lend freely; it is even less likely to take extra risk to help if the borrower gets into trouble. Respect helps in other aspects of the relationship too.

The chemistry must apply to more than just individuals. It may be enough in a transaction to respect the professional providing the product, without respecting the rest of his/her firm – barely enough.

A relationship is longer term, involves more areas of the bank, and must continue when the relationship manager changes. The client need not feel close to every single person it deals with; it must feel there are standards of competence and integrity that apply to the bank as a whole, not just to one individual.

Again, the reverse is true. Banks usually deal mainly with the financial staff, sometimes just the treasury staff at large companies. They must, however, have at least a general feeling that the financial people represent the standards of the company as a whole; that what they promise is in line with management's views.

Trust usually takes time to build. Banks must be prepared to take this time; companies must recognise that they have to make some level of commitment to allow the process to work.

Integrity; a long view; seeing the other side's point of view

Relationships require integrity from both sides. An example of lack of integrity in clients, which enrages banks, is to take an idea from one bank and then do the business with another bank. It will damage an existing relationship and stop a developing one in its tracks.

Of course the situation may not be clear cut. The idea may not be as innovative as the bank thinks; or the client may recognise the value of the idea but doubt the ability of the presenting bank to carry it through; or there may be other reasons justifying what looks like dubious behaviour. A company sensitive about its own as well as other people's integrity will usually recognise when something seems dubious. It can of course shrug and say 'not my problem'. In some cases this may be justified; in most, the company has an interest, as well as a moral obligation, in clarifying the situation. If it is satisfied that it is behaving ethically in giving the business to another bank, it should take the trouble to explain why, and listen to the counter arguments. Sometimes, it may offer the bank a co-lead with the client's chosen bank; at others a fee for the idea.

Again, integrity cuts both ways. A bank that makes a big palaver about its 'proprietary' product knowing that it is no such thing deserves to lose both the business and the relationship.

Much the same applies to a borrower and its bank. To conceal weakness, and particularly trouble – or the extent of that trouble – will soon lose support from banks, and deservedly so.

Integrity is allied to, but not always the same as, taking a long view. Integrity may have short term costs but gives long term benefits. But the long term view is inherent in any relationship. It means, on both sides, ensuring that short term costs or profits do not override longer term considerations.

Another way of looking at this is the recognition of value. A bank may recognise what is important to the client, and stretch to provide it even if it does not suit its strategy. The client in return must decide what is valuable to it, what merely convenient; if it insists on the latter, it uses up credibility, and the bank may be less willing next time.

Some banks, in medium term lending, lay great stress on amortisation and covenants. Some do this by rote, and do not really understand the importance or value to themselves, nor to the client. In these cases the client is fully entitled to reject them. However, there are strong arguments in favour of both; properly designed and adapted to the borrower's needs, they can help it almost as much as the bank. In dealing with these arguments, too many clients are dogmatically negative. Often the best banks then stay out of their credit, or come in reluctantly, for small amounts, leaving a weak syndicate. Apart from any loss of prestige, the danger of a weak syndicate soon becomes obvious if anything goes wrong.

Where the bank is able to insist, the company is fighting on the wrong ground, and may have to take whatever covenants the bank requires. An intelligent approach would make the banks define exactly what they want to achieve, and then negotiate covenants that cause the least disruption, and most benefit, to the borrower (see Chapter 9). A sound approach to relationships makes this easy.

The most important form of value in lending, however, is the presence of a particular bank. Companies put great weight on this, for many reasons. One, in recessionary conditions, is to ensure the bank's support if they run into trouble. This requires a bank that will keep its own credit rating, and take a calm view of problem loans and the risks of dealing with them. Companies that want this often illogically insist on the price offered by banks which do not match these criteria. And yet profitable lending on a sound credit basis is still crucial to a bank's viability, and confidence in the basis of the credit the best argument for supporting a troubled borrower.

Open information, and understanding, both ways

A major barrier to the development of quality relationships is secrecy. The damage is most obvious in lending, particularly medium to long term. Too many companies expect their banks to make a long term judgement about their credit, but refuse the information on which the bank could base that judgement.

It is unwise to expect a bank to support a troubled company that has systematically withheld information. How far to support a troubled company is always a difficult judgement. The easy way out for a bank is to say 'no new money, and pay me or I sue'. It is not always the way to get the most back, but it carries the least risk of increasing the loss, or of being a shadow director. To eschew the easy way out, the bank needs confidence in management. This has been undermined by the mere fact that the company is in trouble. The impact is less if management has foreseen the trouble, advised the bank in advance of the threat, and discussed possible solutions. This enables the bank to test these solutions and satisfy itself that they make sense and give it the best chance of getting its money back.

A bank that learns overnight of a borrower's trouble must wonder why; whether management knows why; what management is doing about the problem, and the chances of success; and whether management is even now telling the whole story. This does not help constructive risk taking.

Transaction borrowers are likely to have a wide range of lenders, most of whom know little about, and have little or no loyalty to, the borrower. Such a company needs a lead bank, which may be supported (or hindered) by some form of committee, has a massive task, and runs legal risks. Unless it can gain the confidence of the banks it is unlikely to have much chance of saving the company. But the confidence it can instil must be as much based on its knowledge of the company and trust in management as on the bank's own competence. A trustworthy bank will not persuade other banks to take steps in which it itself has no confidence. Even where it knows the company's business well, it is likely to have to take much on trust itself; to persuade others to follow in these circumstances is a major step and a major risk if the act of faith proves unjustified. Moreover, for reasons which only a psychiatrist can explain, banks in these conditions are always more inclined to lash out at the lead bank than at the borrower. So, if you are looking to your bank to lead a rescue, make sure you keep it well informed.

But information is not only useful in credit. Banks cannot provide companies with the product they need, or with advice, without information about the company's business and finances. They may still provide the company with what it wants, but companies are not always the best judge of what they need, particularly in times that are more difficult than they are willing to recognise.

Credit standing and credit consciousness

All companies need banks, and all except the very weakest credits should be able to borrow, at least up to a point. So credit standing is not an absolute requirement, except at the bottom of the scale. Not all banks choose to lend to all levels of credit quality, however. Those that do apply different criteria to different levels of credit risk.

Companies need to know what their own credit quality is therefore. They also need to be conscious of what will change that credit quality – or has changed it, in some cases – and of the impact of such a change. This applies equally whatever the direction of the change.

A company that was AAA rated five years ago, but is now a declining A fools itself if it expects unchanged treatment. It must expect to pay a higher rate, give more in the way of covenants, etc. The same applies the other way. A former weak B, which is now an improving BB+, should get entirely better treatment from its banks. A good relationship bank will offer this treatment, but will probably be a little behind the rate of improvement in the credit.

Banks must also be conscious of their own credit. Again this cuts both ways. The small band of AAA banks hold their status in part because they are well capitalised, in part because they earn a good return on that capital, and in part for a variety of other reasons individual to each bank. But the need for capital and a return mean that a cheap bank is rarely a good one. Moreover, there is a scarcity value to an AAA rating. If a company wants to do a 10 year swap, it may want the security of an AAA counterparty; so do many others, and the bank has limits set by its capital to how many swaps it can do, and what it must earn on them.

Friendship, not marriage

The recognition that a relationship is not exclusive is important. Companies need more than one bank to provide the range of skills to cover their needs. They also need the competition among relationship banks to ensure that they get the quality service they pay for. No bank should object to this, providing the company treats its relationship banks fairly. Fairly need not mean equally, but it must mean openly, and with proper credit to each bank for its efforts.

Banks also have more than one client. Often these compete with each other, sometimes they want to take each other over. Normal competition should be no problem. There is no reason for a reputable bank to betray the confidence of one client to another, and every reason not to do so. Nor is there any reason for a bank that develops a novel product to confine it to one client. However, if the client brings the idea to the bank, then it is entitled to ask the bank to keep it confidential, at least until it is in the marketplace.

Acquisitions are more difficult. In the extreme case a bank with one client trying to take over another may have to disqualify itself from acting for either, whether advising or lending. However, for a bank to do this is a considerable sacrifice. Acquisitions and their financing are among the most profitable pieces of banking business; moreover, if other banks work with the acquirer, they have the inside track for a lead relationship with the merged company.

A full chapter would be needed to do justice to the complexities of the subject of acquisitions, allowing for: the relative profitability of the two accounts; whether the bank has information critical to either side; whether its role is key to the success of one party; or whether it is passing up a good opportunity for reasons that make no difference to the outcome, and many other factors. Here we will only say that the bank needs to have a strategy, and an ethical framework for dealing with these situations, and to be prepared to explain the strategy. Indeed it may well be sensible to make its general approach known before any specific case arises.

Acquisitions can be very emotional affairs, but companies need to recognise that any bank can be put in a difficult position. The mere fact that a bank does business with a company that is bidding for you does not make it somehow evil. If you believe in the value of your relationship with a bank, you must recognise that the bank places value on all its relationships. If the other company is more valuable to it than you are, that is more your fault than the bank's. And particularly if you have withheld information, you have taken away from the bank what is often the prime argument that it should not support the other side.

In other words, friendship has limits and varying intensities and so do relationships. A bank or a company that fails to recognise this will probably fail to realise the maximum benefits from its relationships. But loyalty is part of friendship. You do not let a friend down if you can help it, and you expect that he or she will not let you down. If you are forced to choose between friends you do so in the least hurtful way possible.

8 Developing corporate relationships: the bank viewpoint

As pointed out in Chapter 7, each bank's approach to corporate relationships stems basically from its perception of itself. In short, a bank will have to identify correctly its particular skills and any comparative advantages it may possess, whether in structured lending, special products, funding or research. Its approach to the corporate field will, of course, have been influenced by its own historical development and those relationships which have accrued to the organisation over time, from geographical setting or historical business mix. Understanding those factors leads to the bank's strategy described at length above, giving the institution an overall policy and set of objectives. These will encompass the business areas to be stressed, i.e. where its future growth is expected to come from. That consideration, and the consequent marketing effort, immediately bring up the question of funding, no longer to be taken for granted in the 1990s, when liquidity may not be so freely available to a bank as before.

One of those overall objectives may well be to develop corporate relationships, but not in every case. Some banks have been set up purely to develop retail business, others to offer advice to high net worth individuals. Promotion of corporate business may be a little diffuse in large banks which have many business areas and a wide geographic spread. It is easier to see the concept in the case of a newly established bank, which may want to stress corporate banking as the core of its efforts. Indeed, the author of this chapter set up such a bank in London in the 1980s with the specific purpose of dealing with multinational clients in Europe and elsewhere. This forced us to think through how one develops corporate clients as a new entrant to the market, representing a foreign parent not from the banking sector and having no customer base here at all. Some of this chapter relates to that experience in developing a strategy to obtain corporate relationships in a world which has become increasingly over-banked, where many large corporates are themselves cash rich and highly expert in financial markets, and against a background in which securitisation has meant less dependence upon banks for corporate funding generally.

Selection of types of customers

After a bank has tried to identify its own particular skills and services, it will then need to select the right kinds of corporate customers. It makes little sense, for example, to decide to be a major player in a specific currency, if one then finds out that few, if any, corporates have important foreign exchange transactions to settle or to hedge in that currency. (One could also find that the market in that currency is dominated by a handful of powerful trading banks, with huge customer and intercompany flows already, and that the average transaction amount is far beyond its own scale.)

It would be foolhardy to enter that situation as a market maker, hoping to win corporate accounts as a result. It is difficult anyway to start off at the top end of the scale with the largest corporates, either in size of credit offered or technical services. To expect to be a meaningful house bank for a large multinational company implies the ability to supply very large amounts of credit, often with little notice and without a committed facility, and ready advice on market movements and trends around the world. It can mean dealing at non-market times for such clients, such as late on Friday when they might want to close out transactions when the financial markets are thin or closed.

The first task of banking tactics in the corporate area is thus to pinpoint which customers to solicit. In other words, the bank will need to target potential corporate clients whose profiles match its own objectives. The bank should avoid stressing the size of a corporate target for its own sake, but be realistic about what it can legitimately offer and which companies it can realistically approach. Its approach can of course be ameliorated by services offered by other parts of its group, if it represents a large and multipartite financial group. Underwriting or stock exchange listing by a sister or parent company, or outstanding research capacity, offer obvious entries to a potential customer already enjoying benefits from those services.

Need for differentiation

There are some 500 banks in London alone, with every possible kind of structure and product range. Whether new or well established, a bank must differentiate itself from the others in order to attract any consideration at all from those corporate treasurers it wishes to approach.

Differentiation can take many forms. Among these are:

(a) Special knowledge of one area or industry.
(b) Cheaper pricing.
(c) Expertise in handling actual transactions.
(d) Problem solving ability, etc.

Specialised knowledge

Specialised knowledge can be an excellent tactical advantage. For example, for several years Japan has been perhaps the world's richest country, measured by balance of payments surpluses and resultant capital outflows; even in the difficult times of the mid-1990s, Japan has become a source of great liquidity for the world, both for the US government and many sovereign borrowing agencies, and for the private sector. No treasurer of a large company can afford to overlook the financing potential of Japan; he or she will wish to be kept current on that by banks with expert knowledge of the Japanese economy. Indeed, a corporate treasurer can possibly be induced to open a relationship and give a new bank worthwhile business in return for accurate and continued information on Japanese market conditions and, extrapolated, how Japan's flows affect other markets. The same is true for advice on the US and certain European markets. Even an infinitesimal shift of a large corporate's short term market transactions, say in the money market area, can be valuable to the aspiring bank. (It goes without saying that the bank needs to offer market rates in such cases.) Similar in-depth knowledge can likewise attract new clients dealing directly or indirectly with specific industries. One thinks here of the investment banks with their specialised knowledge: project finance in several cases, Scandinavia/shipping in others, or the Middle East.

Cheaper pricing

This is one tactic used by certain banks to gain clients and market share. However, this tactic is unlikely to be successful in the long term when applied to corporate marketing. Many treasurers may well take advantage of inexpensive sources of funds, particularly in times of tighter liquidity. But they rarely respect a bank which simply is a low cost provider and brings little else to the party. If the client becomes cash rich, or indeed the willingness of the bank in question to provide low cost funding dries up, little is left on which to base or maintain any relationship. Loss leaders put the bank into the category of a dull commodity provider at best. Market share strategies are anyway misguided and chimerical.

Expertise in handling actual transactions

Some banks have built up effective and long lasting corporate relationships by being efficient low cost providers of transactional services. In the 1970s banks set up cash management teams in order to help treasurers reduce their float and transaction costs. The best of these also developed excellent software systems which treasurers could use for on-line control and rapid transmission of their international payments and receipts, and the resulting exposures. Bank of America has been particularly successful in this regard, winning and keeping a large number of UK corporate relationships through its operational capabilities, even when its headquarters in California was undergoing a severe liquidity squeeze and eventual downsizing.

Problem solving ability

Undoubtedly the best tactic and by far the most difficult one to implement is to differentiate oneself by problem solving ability. There are too many banks and bankers offering ordinary products, generally at about the same price. No matter how well versed corporates are in financial markets and risk management, they will still respond to advisory services dealing with the many complexities of a corporate treasurer's responsibilities. These span all of the main pillars of treasury management: interest rate management, foreign exchange risk and long term structure of the balance sheet. Depending on the size and expertise of the respective client, a bank whose strategy is based on good advisory services can offer assistance along the whole spectrum of risk management.

For the smaller or newly international customer it can help with definition and identification of exposures *per se* and assessment of future risks. For the more sophisticated customer, the bank can devise methods for hedging or concoct specific products, usually options based, which precisely fit that company's needs. In this regard, some of the banks making rapid inroads into new corporate relationships in the 1990s are those developing exactly such specialised hedging products such as 'look back' options and 'knock-out' options, where there is no quoted market and only a small number of players. They emulate the historical success of the British merchant banks, which had always lived on their wits and problem solving abilities, rather than capital base or branch networks. Sadly as we saw in Chapter 3 the old style of merchant banking is giving way to capital intensive investment banking.

Knowledge of the target company

The problem solving approach in particular, but indeed any corporate marketing strategy, involves very deep understanding of a corporate client's own structure, management and financial positions. This, of course, should be the aim of any serious banker, whether coming from investment banking or commercial banking. Customer knowledge involves far more than simply reading financial statements and reports about the industry; it means visits to the company, ideally the manufacturing sites as well as headquarters. It means winning the trust of the company; management should share with bank partners their aspirations and concerns about future growth, revenues and financial structure. The trust thereby developed amounts to insider knowledge in the very best sense of that word, providing a platform on which better advice can be structured. Only if the bank fully understands the company's basic financial position and risks, and its attitude towards risk, can it develop appropriate and reasonable funding and hedging strategies as outlined above.

It may seem overly grandiose for a bank to expect to come up with good risk management or other advice which existing house banks have not, but this is not impossible. Sophisticated risk management techniques are constantly being developed by both corporations and banks; while not patentable or secret very long, they do allow a bank to hand-tailor products of considerable value, despite its size or newness. Not a lot of people are necessary, just some bright, numerate and problem solving ones. Indeed, a bank specialising in the development of risk management programmes can easily, and legitimately, take what it has learned from solving one set of corporate problems or risks and apply that knowledge to other situations. A bank may also be able to suggest new types of funding through its own special placing power or its awareness of credit from new sources, probably geographically new as well. A treasurer wishing to deepen and diversify a company's sources of funding will listen carefully to such arguments. From the treasurer's point of view, structural funding arrangements must also be guarded and monitored continuously, given the state of flux in the banking industry nowadays.

Bank/corporate relationships thus are much deeper than is commonly believed; a depth of understanding is engendered which goes both ways. A bank should be willing to share with its corporate clientele the same kind of information, i.e. its own aspirations, the broad outlines of its strategy for the future and its own likely balance sheet and funding structure. While this has always been true, it seems much more important now, when many banks have suffered steady losses in lending books and have often undergone subsequent downgrading of their credit rating. In numerous cases, a bank's credit standing will no longer be as good as that of the corporate customer from which it is soliciting business; it is important to be upfront about such matters. Such bilateral knowledge of each other is a long term process requiring regular and continuous exchange of information and contacts. It is of course meant to form the basis of a permanent relationship which will warrant the high costs to banks of marketing personnel, credit analysis and business trips. Banks expanding or setting out along the lines of this strategy should be prepared to wait for results, only little by little expecting to develop the trust and thus the profitable business which good corporate relationships can bring.

Implicit in all the above is a thorough understanding of the industry the target company is in, its relative position in size and technology, the quality of its management (also *vis-à-vis* that of its competitors) and the direction the industry is going. The considerable effort taken to understand the industry will reward itself in being able to understand the customer's needs better, and also in helping to pick those companies surging ahead as opposed to lagging behind (or fizzling out) in their industry. It would be invidious to name here the numerous household names, once industry leaders and sought after by banks, which have spectacularly foundered on the back of unsound and insupportable expansion plans. (Aesop's fable about the frog puffing itself up in great pride, until it exploded, told the same story 2000 years ago.)

Finally, a bank's own strong credit status, if it still has one, can nowadays be a good selling point. Corporate treasurers want to be able to depend upon their banks, and indefinitely. In recent medium term syndications, the corporate borrower has more carefully vetted suggested syndicate members, on the basis of creditworthiness, than before. If its suppliers disappear or withdraw from international lending, then the firm's own ability to count on such banks for funding when needed is diminished.

Pitfalls

The above framework is somewhat theoretical. It can take nearly infinite patience to work out such a long strategy in practice. It is hard enough simply to get access to treasurers these days, who will not spend a lot of hours with bankers passing the time of day. Contacts should only be requested when the bank has something of value to say. Treasurers may eventually try out banks in the really tough areas (Eastern European or African export financing for example), or in low profit, labour intensive business. It can take a very long time before insight into their real problems and risks is granted. To state the obvious again, loss leader pricing is unlikely to advance a bank very far along this process. Conversely, a bank should try to develop a sense of when a relationship is never going to materialise; if this is the conclusion, the bank should not waste further time on futile marketing.

Some of the biggest and most sophisticated banks have built in profit centre accounting in order to evaluate the value of customer relationships, even down to products offered by the customer. Serious profit centre analysis will show a bank quickly not only where it stands with each customer, but also which products are most valuable in its longer term strategy. This numerate approach is important in the essential stage of monitoring a relationship carefully.

Methods of approach

A further tactic for the banks to devise is how best to approach a prospective corporate customer, which will undoubtedly have several, maybe even too many, bank relationships already. Indeed, a number of corporates seem to be actively reducing bank relationships by weeding out weaker or non-performing banks. The chief executive of the company, often known to the chief executive or chairman of the bank, could seem an obvious person to approach. While he or she may give an introduction down the line, it is a rare chief executive who will impose a new banking relationship on the chief financial officer or treasurer. The approach is best made to the people who will be responsible for the relationship. This will mostly be the treasurer, or assistant treasurer, but might start off with a corporate dealer, if the bank has dealt with treasury products and market advice as its entry into the company.

Negotiations after relationships are started

Starting a relationship is one thing; maintaining and deepening that relationship through the many and varied negotiations that will occur over time is quite another. Negotiations over credit, whether about structure or cost, or over extension of new treasury products or new operating services, always involve some give and take on both sides. Each counterpart needs to recognise the other's bottom line; this is helped by the knowledge of each other's strengths and weaknesses as recommended above. While flexibility is obviously needed, either side should be prepared to withdraw from a particular transaction if the price is not within its range of tolerance. Occasional missed deals for price reasons will not usually cause a permanent rift between bank and client, especially if openly explained. However, more long lasting inability to agree on pricing or provision of new credit/services indicates a more serious problem and threat to the relationship. This should be openly faced and mutually discussed. If the bank does not wish to offer credit at market rates, then it should probably consider severing the relationship (see Chapter 10) If the corporate customer is prospering and the bank is being recalcitrant, then the firm should consider winding up the relationship.

Finally, negotiations require a team approach. Despite the nature of the transactions being negotiated – structured finance, derivative products, a netting service, or whatever – the bank's team should always include one banker familiar with and to the customer, who knows its activities well. Indeed, this caveat justifies the role of the 'relationship banker', recently maligned as good old Charlie, who wears white shoes and plays golf with his clients. The good relationship banker is the vehicle through which the relationship flows, the repository of knowledge about the customer and the giver of knowledge about the bank, the leader of the negotiating team. The time of the relationship banker has come again, while the transaction-oriented hot shots – short termists one and all – are folding their tents and slinking away.

9 Maintaining and reviewing banking relationships

So far, we have been discussing the background and theory of banking relationships and the underlying policy from both the corporate and banking viewpoint. Now it is time to consider some practical examples.

Before that, however, it is worth reviewing how banking relationships go wrong. What are the commonest problems?

(a) The maturity profile of strategic decision making is very different between companies and banks. The company building a factory or launching a new product is looking at a five to ten year time horizon, whereas a bank operates in a 'money' environment, which is essentially very short term.

(b) Failure to understand these differences together with those of objectives and policies is a common problem.

(c) Failure to communicate on matters such as change of organisation or policy leads to suspicion. Financial decisions are sometimes taken outside the bank at local level and sometimes even outside the country. These can render the bank strategy obsolete with immediate effect.

(d) Similarly on the corporate side an abrupt change in circumstances, e.g. performance of the company, will soon alarm the bank. A 'no surprises' policy has everything to recommend it.

(e) Finally the desire to dominate the relationship will soon lead to problems.

As we saw in Chapter 5, both sides need to be quite clear why they are doing business with each other; there needs to be a clear statement of what each is looking for from the relationship, which in some ways should be regarded as a partnership. This is always more difficult for the bank, since it has to make a difficult choice between possible loss making services now, against lucrative returns in the future.

Banking relationships are therefore often seen as adversarial. Most of the time they chug along in a rather reactive even negative way until something dramatic happens, e.g. a takeover, the company getting into trouble, or a major change in policy on the part of the bank. It is strange that in so many other areas of business the relationship between supplier and customer is often one of partnership, where matters such as price, delivery and quality are under continuous discussion. It does not help, of course, that there are so many bankers offering much the same product, so competition is naturally fierce and the potential to differentiate somewhat limited. After all, which company would enter a market where there can be as many as 500 competing organisations offering roughly the same product?

The case study material that follows examines all these trends and surely has lessons for both sides of the relationship. There are three case studies: Bricom, Federal-Mogul and Cookson.

Bricom was a highly geared and complex buyout in which the negotiation and implementation of the undertakings in the financing arrangements, specifically covenants, occupied a significant amount of the treasurer's time. Federal-Mogul is a US corporation which found its expansion plans hindered by credit rating downgradings and difficulty in building a successful banking syndicate. The Cookson Group is a UK multinational which after financial difficulties some years ago, has developed a formal banking charter.

Judith Harris-Jones, now of Arthur Andersen, then newly appointed treasurer of a buyout company, relates her experience of the early days of Bricom. This case study underlines the need to pay close attention to loan agreements and specifically the proposed covenants. The problem, as we saw in Chapter 7, is not that bankers want to prevent the company from operating effectively – and therefore profitably – but they do want to protect the banks' money. Bankers often use standard clauses which do not fit all circumstances and they are tempted to cover everything – the 'kitchen sink' syndrome. The Bricom deal was a complicated buyout but as Judith Harris-Jones points out, it could have gone more smoothly had all parties adopted a more pragmatic view. In other words, less 'we always do it this way' and more 'what are we trying to achieve?'

The Bricom case

Notwithstanding the shifts in perspective necessitated by evolving markets and the credit being represented in that market, experience suggests that there are some continuing themes in the conduct of successful banking relationships. Successful in this context denotes a positive commercial outcome for both bankers and banked; it specifically does not mean screwing charges and margins down to paper thin levels, nor does it imply tying struggling businesses into legal strait-jackets which reduce normal operating activity to the status of events of default.

The recognition by both bank and corporate that they are mutually dependent for success must be the first requirement for good banking relationships. On the bank's side this means developing a thorough understanding of its customers, markets, management and culture, and the financial imperatives implied by its corporate strategy. (The treasurer should insist on no less a level of effort by its bankers.) The corporate treasurer also has a responsibility to understand the business in which his/her company is, or wishes to become, involved. This point is not made lightly; many treasurers construe their role as an outward facing officer of the company, an interface between the consolidated balance sheet and the financial community. While the importance of this aspect is not to be underestimated, it is a necessary but not sufficient condition for the successful conduct of banking relationships. To manage the financial risks of a business, it is necessary to under-stand the commercial issues and exposures; credibility with the banking sector will only be earned by those who demonstrate this knowledge. A side benefit of this approach is that the standing of the treasurer with his commercial colleagues will also improve, thus enhancing the contribution the treasurer can make to the company's overall financial performance.

In addition to the respect accorded to the treasurer who has a broad understanding of all the issues determining the company's future, further points will be awarded by the bank if it feels dealings are open, honest and straightforward. To establish this confidence, the treasurer must at all times be proactive but especially when the company is under pressure. If the bank senses that its customer is withholding information, or circumventing any of its formal or informal obligations to lenders, 'you and I are in this together' (so tenuously built up over years) will instantly become 'us and them'.

While a borrower may feel justifiably irritated by all the destructive and time-wasting activity that is the consequence of a collapse in confidence, the clever treasurer will recognise the danger, and manage matters accordingly. Being right is no antidote to being insolvent.

In 1988 I left Rolls Royce to join the Bricom Group Ltd. Rolls Royce had recently been privatised, and from the banking viewpoint had been transformed from a triple A government credit to a private sector business with a worldwide reputation, a strong balance sheet and a sound order book. The company had been able to write its own term sheets and documentation for the refinancing that accompanied flotation, and achieve the best terms seen in the market up till then.

Bricom was about to become a highly leveraged buyout, with a gearing of either 99:1 or 90:10, depending on the definition of equity and the definition of gearing. It is difficult to say whether the lenders or I got the greatest shock when the troops gathered for the first round of negotiations. While I readily appreciated that the lending margins would be different from those that I had become used to (150 basis points compared with 10), I was not prepared for the bankers' apparent assumption that their terms and conditions would be more or less imposed on Bricom. Regardless of the credit rating of the borrower, it is surely against the interests of all parties to agree to terms that constrain the company from making commercially effective decisions, or structuring its business and finances so as to minimise interest tax and currency exposures. Yet in circumstances where the lenders suspect the security on which they have agreed to rely may not be adequate to pay the piper should the tune be called, the additional safeguards that are sought often seem to condemn the borrower to operate less efficiently than they might. I found this difficult to accept from a commercial perspective; the debate took us into the early (and, indeed, late) hours of several mornings. At the closing, I had been unable to achieve the balance of power I had really wanted; nevertheless we have a more practical agreement, and one that recognised the rapid pattern of change which was likely to ensue at Bricom, than we might otherwise have been committed to.

The treasurer of a highly geared business can accept that the lenders wish to ensure there are no authorised changes to capital structure, and that no dividends are paid to shareholders without the banks' consent. It seems reasonable for the banks to wish to agree budgets and see management accounts promptly. The financial covenants and repayment schedules should be demanding since management is faced with a challenging task, and only a superior performance justifies the risk being taken. However, in my experience, the banks' stringent criteria of comprehensiveness and materiality may frustrate that very performance.

For instance, the principle of taking security over everything is a costly one, in terms of money, management time, and in some cases, business activity. In the case of Bricom, a conglomerate with 300 subsidiaries grouped into 25 businesses, operating in 40 countries, it would surely have been better to apply the 80:20 rule, saving expense, but securing the most valuable assets – after all, the execution of a mortgage does not generate a pro rata fee. It was even suggested that all the cash flows generated by the businesses should be sorted through a holding account with the agent bank, in order that security could be protected – imagine the cost in paperwork and float! In some cases the execution of security is directly counterproductive, alienating local management and prejudicing local reputations, particularly where the success of a business is more dependent on its people than its tangible assets. This point holds true for the furnishing of cross-guarantees, the execution of which has caused precious teams of people to decamp with their skills. The preoccupation with security has led banks to impose inefficient cash management and tax structures, because they fear that shifting assets between locations would remove those assets from their grasp. In the wake of the 1990–93 recession, banks may have discovered that security is not what it seems; to my recent knowledge some still prefer the illusion of a charge rather than to rely on the reality of management or cash flow.

Once security is in place, 'consent' becomes the name of the game. Anything that is not in the normal course of business requires prior written consent, lest it detract from the value of the assets. In a group that relies for its commercial rationale on restructuring and rationalisation this becomes an onerous task. Over a period of two years we wrote 300 letters to the agent bank requesting consent for disposals, mergers of group companies, acquisitions of minority shareholdings, restructuring balance sheets of thinly capitalised businesses and creating tax efficient organisational structures. Sometimes we had to request waivers of events of default, because small companies in far flung locations had entered into arrangements entirely in keeping with local practice, but which could be interpreted as the creation of an indemnity or the establishment of a facility – neither of which was permitted. In retrospect, the scope of our obligations was so broad, and the materiality so tightly drawn, that we were probably in default most of the time, even though the thoroughness and integrity of management was not in doubt. Is this in the banks' interest? Would they not be better to rely more on their own judgement of management's abilities, and structure a deal that delegates more of the management responsibility? Failing this, the borrower must negotiate as cogently as possible for a sensible level of materiality.

My experience as a corporate treasurer, from and during my time as a consultant to companies in deep water with their bankers, has led me to realise that when companies are not in strong enough positions to structure their own loan agreements, banks rely heavily on their lawyers in framing documentation; and that lawyers rely heavily on the deals they have done previously. The structure they put forward may or may not suit your business needs; more likely, not. At Bricom, we spent so much time sorting out the senior, or acquisition debt, that we had left little time to put the working capital facilities in place.

Since only the practical borrowing arrangements would differ from the documentation for the senior debt, it seemed a straight-forward proposition; however, on first reading it became clear that the lawyers' idea of how a multinational on a tight budget should operate its overdrafts did not accord with a treasurer's . I have since seen multinationals manoeuvred into arrangements which were clearly against their own and the bankers' interests; presumably because in the stress of the moment, the commercial objectives became submerged in the sea of legalese.

It is therefore important, as a treasurer, not to lose your cool professional head when all about you may be losing theirs. Once the loan agreements are in place, it is too late to start negotiating.

The Federal-Mogul case[1]

Brad Asher, a financial journalist based in Chicago, wrote this case study about Federal-Mogul's search for committed banks. It illustrates two key factors in banking relationships. First, how difficult they become when the company suffers a credit rating downgrading. As we saw before, banks have become highly sensitive to the credit analysis process. When credit ratings are public, the sensitivity is heightened and banks usually have precise rules governing acceptability of ratings. (Corporates adopt the same approach to banks with regard to deposits or bank paper.) Second, the case shows the need for great thought in selecting banks for a syndicate, bearing in mind also that syndicated banking can be seen as the opposite of relationship banking. The company needs to be certain that the bank will be able to deliver what is required both

[1]This case study appears with the permission of the Economist Intelligence Unit.

domestically and internationally. *Ad hoc* syndicates seldom work and when the going gets tough there is a rush for the door. Companies therefore need to spend as much time choosing banks as they do for other suppliers ranging from components to advertising services.

Federal-Mogul's search for committed banks

Try building solid banking relationships when your company is labouring under a load of debt and your industry is in deep trouble. That's just what American car parts maker Federal-Mogul has been struggling to do with only varying degrees of success for more than two years.

Federal-Mogul's core bank group began to melt following the company's downgrade from single A to triple B in late 1990. This was triggered in part by the company's acquisition of Glyco, a German engine-bearing manufacturer. The purchase was made when the American car market was crashing, which left the company with more debt than its bankers deemed prudent. Bankers were particularly unhappy that the company violated covenants in its revolving credit facility to make the purchase.

Not surprisingly, Federal-Mogul received a less than warm reception when it had to amend the covenant of that agreement in early 1991. The agent bank said it wanted out of the revolving facility even though it was not due for review for many months. Burdened with its own balance sheet problems, the bank felt that getting involved in a new loan with Federal-Mogul was too risky.

The withdrawal of the agent forced Federal-Mogul to begin the process of renegotiating a new $150 million revolving credit with a new, more stable core of banks. This has been an arduous, unfinished job not only because of Federal-Mogul's strained finances. The company has unusually difficult requirements to meet at a time when American banks are under pressure from regulators to strengthen their loan portfolios and improve their capital adequacy.

Federal-Mogul needs banks that understand and accept the cyclical and long term risks of the car industry. It also wants banks that are committed to its strategy for repositioning the company in that stricken industry, including its growing commitment to expanding internationally. The firm, which does about one-third of its $1 billion in sales outside the USA, has been making strategic acquisitions in Europe and needs to enlarge its global network of banks. To complicate matters further, Federal-Mogul is also trying to lessen its dependence on bank financing.

International help

In seeking to establish a new revolving credit, Federal-Mogul invited bids from 30 banks plus the members of the old revolving credit. When the dust settled in the autumn of 1991, a new core of banks had been put together that was much more international than the original group. Four of the nine banks that participated in the previous revolving credit withdrew.

They were replaced by banks that had grown in importance to the company in recent years, in part as a result of its expanding international business. Union Bank of Switzerland had already lent Federal-Mogul short term financing; the Bank of New York had also provided funding for overseas operations. Nippon Credit was recruited by Chemical Bank, which became the new agent bank following its merger with Manufacturers Hanover Trust, long a banking partner of Federal-Mogul. The company also strengthened its international connection by arranging a new $59 million Deutschmark-denominated term loan, which was led by the German bank BHF, in order to help finance Glyco operations in Europe.

American banks in the consortium also included NBD, Comerica and Manufacturers National. Based in Detroit, they have strong ties to the car industry and had participated in the original revolving credit. Continental Bank was able to persuade the company that it understood both the industry and the company's needs. 'They had done their homework and want in' explains David Benton, Federal-Mogul's treasury manager. The new nine member group was rounded out by Royal Bank of Canada, which has long provided local financing and cash management services to Federal-Mogul's Canadian operations.

Tough terms

The company's slumping credit rating forced it to emphasise bank willingness over pricing on the new revolver. 'Pricing in 1991 was secondary to credit availability,' says Mr Benton. 'Every time we went to the table, we were on negative credit watch.' The firm's credit rating was knocked down again to double B in December 1991. The best it could get on pricing was a graduated pricing schedule. The margin over LIBOR goes down as the company improves its fixed charge coverage.

Federal-Mogul also accepted restrictions on dividend payments. The company cannot pay over $12 million in annual dividends unless annualised net earnings available to common shareholders exceed $15 million. Such conditions may seem tough, but they are in line wiith the higher prices American banks are charging. Banks have boosted prices to ensure an adequate risk-adjusted return on equity in order to comply with capital adequacy requirements.

While Federal-Mogul has very little leverage to haggle over borrowing charges, it's a different story with off-balance sheet, fee-based services. Here the firm can extact some pricing concessions by shopping around. Its strategy is to offer the business to its relationship banks as a reward for their participation in credit facilities. But it offers the business on a competitive bid basis.

For example, it invited bids from four of its core banks on its American cash management business. It wanted to replace its previous cash management bank, which has left the core group of lenders. Since the company perceived that there was very little difference in the quality of service they all offered, price was the principal criterion for awarding the contract.

A global network

Federal-Mogul has been most successful in building a strong international network. With the withdrawal of a major international bank from the original lending group, the company had to replace its banking connections in Taiwan and Malaysia. The Bank of New York was able to provide credit arrangements in Asia since its international presence had increased after the acquisition of Irving Trust.

Federal-Mogul's need for banks with international presence had risen substantially after the Glyco acquisition. That gave the company a big manufacturing operation in Germany and made it the largest engine-bearing producer in Europe. The firm chose BHF and Union Bank of Switzerland as its primary banks in Europe. BHF has a long relationship with Glyco, and Union Bank added capital market expertise.

Federal-Mogul expects its financial needs in Europe to grow. The company would like to transfer American-style consolidated funding to Europe through a centralised finance company. A finance company could raise money more cheaply by going directly to capital markets.

As part of this financial strategy Federal-Mogul would want to arrange financial commitments from its European banks to support a finance company. 'I will always need local collection and local overdraft lines,' says Mr Benton. 'But I will also need banks that will lend $50 million or so to the finance company.'

Testing the commitment

Federal-Mogul's financial plans for Europe illustrate its overall financial strategy; increasing capital market funding while maintaining a reliable stable of banks for essential services and some financing. The company recognises that it needs bank credit to help fund operations and occasionally for fast financing of acquisitions. But it also wants to replace much of its high priced bank credit with capital market financing as soon as possible.

In July 1992 the company had raised $55 million through an innovative trade receivables-backed deal that garnered a triple A rating from Standard and Poors. The proceeds were used to retire the Deutschmark term loan early, saving the company an estimated $2 million in annual interest expense. The company has also bolstered its cash flow by selling off non-core assets. It disposed of its Huck industrial fastenings business, which added enough cash reserves so that it did not need to tap its new credit lines until September 1992.

But reducing reliance on bank financing is proving difficult, as its decision to buy TRW's after-market car parts business for $215 million shows. The company was able to fund only about one-third of the purchase price with an issue of 1.6 million shares of convertible exchangeable preferred stock. Almost two-thirds of the deal was financed by a $20 million draw down of the revolver plus a $125 million six year term loan.

But Federal-Mogul also filed with the Securities and Exchange Commission in February 1993 to sell up to 5.75 million shares of common stock. The proceeds of that sale will be used to retire at least part of the bank debt incurred in the TRW acquisition.

Nevertheless, arranging the term loan showed that the banks' commitment to the company could be fragile. The nine core banks that participated in the new $150 million revolving credit facility were asked to submit bids for the term loan. In addition, invitations were sent out to many of the banks that had participated in the negotiations for the new credit line and to those that had taken part in the Deutschmark loan. Anxious about too many questionable property loans on their books, two of the nine core banks dropped out.

This experience underscores a fundamental problem for Federal-Mogul and many other multinationals. As long as banks are fighting to generate adequate returns, some will be unable to live up to long term commitments even if they make them. Federal-Mogul readily admits that its current core of banks, which it has worked long and hard to build, may not hold together for long.

The Cookson approach to banking relationships

The third case study written by Michael MacCallan, Group
Treasurer of the Cookson Group, is concerned with the
development of a sophisticated relationship banking model. As we
noted earlier in this chapter, many banking relations are passive
until something happens. This is not the case here. The company
learnt from an earlier difficult financial period in which some banks
walked away. The company clearly sees banking relationships as an
essential tool of its corporate strategy and reviews these
relationships regularly and rigorously leaving nothing to chance.
Interestingly, with such a precise charter, the steps towards ending
a relationship are also quite clear. This is the theme for the next
chapter.

About the company

Cookson is the UK-based parent of an international group of
companies which are primarily engaged in the manufacture of
specialist materials and products for use in a broad range of
industries including electronics, steel, plastics, jewellery and
ceramics. Its turnover in 1995 was £1.8 billion. It is divided into five
businesses which are Electronic Materials, Advanced Refractories,
Ceramics Supplies, Engineered Products and Plastics. The Cookson
Group is quoted on the London Stock Exchange and has a market
capitalisation of some £1.8 billion in September 1996. Over the past
few years, Cookson has undergone a fundamental change in both
organisational structure and culture. These changes have enabled
the group treasury to overhaul the group's worldwide treasury
function and secure an enhanced treasury risk management and
control framework.

Banking philosophy and approach

The company's objective for bank relationship management,
approved by the board, is:

> To establish, maintain and develop relationships with a core group of
> international banks to provide the group with long term bank
> support, irrespective of adverse short term business conditions.'

This may well be an objective to which many corporates can
subscribe; putting that objective into practice, however, requires
considerable commitment from a great many people. Whilst it may

be the finance director and the treasurer who develop the philosophy and drive the approach, it also requires 'sign-on' by the group's senior executive management.

Our philosophy has been, and remains, relationship driven. We have selected a small group of major relationship banks, comprising core banks and second tier banks. We keep them fully informed of events at Cookson, with regular opportunities to meet and question the group's senior executive management. We regard the banks as investors in the group, albeit debt investors, and ensure that, as far as we possibly can, they will never be caught unawares by events at the company. In return, we expect continuing support from these banks whether this is in the form of core funding, temporary bridging finance or the normal range of banking services, efficiently and promptly executed and on a cost competitive basis. Whilst we cannot *expect* these banks to support the group through difficult times, we believe that our open approach to bank relationship management helps earn the banks' trust and confidence in both individuals at Cookson and in the group as a whole, so that they would indeed support the company through adverse short term business conditions. Indeed, as noted later, we have had to test this belief in practice.

Whilst our philosophy and approach to bank relationship management has remained in substance the same over the past 10 years, the practical implementation has developed into the 'Cookson's bank charter' which clearly states our commitment to our major relationship banks and what we, in return, expect from them.

The development of relationship banking at Cookson

Whilst we have adopted the relationship (rather than transactional) approach to banking, it has developed over time. The first significant move occurred in the mid-1980s, when the then group treasurer (subsequently the group finance director) arranged bilateral committed facilities with six major banks. Prior to that time, the company's need for such funding was limited; the change in funding requirements was brought about by the acquisition programme.

During the mid/late 1980s, Cookson acquired many companies each with their own banking relationships. At the same time, many banks tried to be 'all things to all corporates'. Together, this meant that the group's operating companies were using a significant number of banks overall, many of which were trying hard to sell products and services, even if the bank itself was not fully capable of providing ongoing support for that service.

The impact of this vast number of banks was partially ameliorated by the group's focusing its use on the six banks providing the bilateral facilities. The financing requirements, however, continued to grow along with the shortening maturity of the existing bilateral facilities. In order to reduce the number of banks used both at group and operating levels, and consolidate the remaining ones, a multiple option finance facility was arranged in 1989, syndicated between 24 committed banks and 12 tender panel banks. The committed portion was for £250 million, whilst the total amount available was £400 million. The facility was structured into three tiers, with Tier 1 representing the group's major relationship banks at the time. During 1990, the group found itself somewhat overgeared, a situation faced by many companies at the time. In September 1990, Cookson's share price fell from 90p to 54p, as a result of an unfavourable rumour circulating in the market at the time. Shortly thereafter, the shares of another large corporate were suspended. The reaction of bankers to the fall in the share price and other (unsubstantiated) market rumours, was split between those that were prepared to support the group and those that were not.

Those banks that knew the group well and with whom we had a close relationship were prepared to support us during our temporary setback. Whilst they did not like the sharp fall in the share price or the high gearing position, the banks had confidence in our finance team to give them an ongoing accurate assessment of the underlying situation and what was being done, through disposals of major non-core businesses, to stabilise and correct the overgearing issue. They could have made our lives extremely difficult. However, the relationship has been built up over several years and the banks, therefore, had had the opportunity to assess the finance team and build up their confidence in them. One interesting comment made by a number of banks after the situation had settled down was that their confidence was maintained not only by their trust in the finance team, but also by the full open dialogue we had with the banks at the time and the fact that we responded immediately to all their questions. Our credibility would have been severely damaged had we tried to withhold information or delay our responses.

The other group of banks, with whom we did not have such a close relationship were not so understanding. Uncommitted lines were withdrawn; indeed one bank with a committed line tried to prevent us from using that line. This group of banks had made up their mind before they had discussed it with us and thus were not prepared to believe anything we said.

Rereading the correspondence from the time is a salutary reminder of how quickly fortunes can be reversed and how you cannot expect banks to continue support; this has to be earned. There are, however, those banks and bankers with whom a relationship is developed over time, allowing trust and confidence to build. Whilst the bank must protect its own shareholders from loss, the relationship at such a crucial time can make or break the situation. It is a cruel lesson of life (and corporate life) that when things go wrong, many other things also start to go wrong at the same time thus having a compounding negative effect. Many a corporate has gone under whilst expecting or assuming bank support and whilst still crying 'it can't happen here'.

By the end of 1990, the group had made asset disposals of some £300 million to bring gearing down to a more manageable level. Furthermore, management changes were introduced which included identifying and developing the group's core businesses on an international basis.

In view of our experience in late 1990 and recognising that the banks themselves were under pressure (through their own bad debt write-offs, restructuring and tight margins), we decided to formalise our relationship philosophy and core banking group. In early 1991, after the situation had stabilised, we met with each of our major banks and discussed with them our intentions to develop the Cookson's bank charter and form a core group of banks. At the same time, we offered to renegotiate margins on our existing bilateral committed facilities. This was partly to acknowledge the support given to us by those banks and partly in recognition of the fact that margins for committed facilities had increased considerably since those facilities were originally negotiated.

From these meetings, we developed Cookson's bank charter, which is discussed in more detail below. We further defined our core banks and our core bank requirements. Since then, with the cancellation of the multi-option facility in 1994, we have restructured our major relationship banks into a small number of core and second tier banks.

Cookson's bank charter

After the meetings with all our major banks in early 1991 we wrote to each of them in May 1991 confirming our philosophy and intention with regard to our bank charter. Our intentions were to:

(a) Form a core group of relationship banks, each bank having a significant committed exposure to the group.
(b) Use these bilateral facilities to fund the group on an ongoing basis. (This would mean that the committed portion of the multi-option facility would revert to being, in the main, a stand-by line.)
(c) Invite the core banks to meet as a group with Cookson's senior executive management, to enable them to know the management and understand the businesses in which the company operates, in more detail.
(d) Invite some or all of the core banks to bid for fee-earning commercial banking/financial business where this might arise and where we believed that particular banks in the core group had the required expertise.
(e) Keep the core banks informed of relevant business opportunities within Cookson (normally with an offer to participate but not to guarantee that they would be given that business).

Those banks that were interested were asked to confirm those specific areas where they felt their organisation had proven capabilities and which, therefore, they would want us to consider when banking- or financial-related projects arose in the future. We wanted to ensure that the core group, as finally formed, had a sufficient range of specialist skills to meet most of our ongoing banking requirements.

The Cookson bank charter was a formalisation of our philosophy and of our previous practice; it was also a statement to other banks that, as we had limited amounts of banking-related business, we wanted to ensure that it was directed to our core banks wherever possible. Given the cancellation of the multi-option facility in 1994, Cookson's bank charter has been extended to include our second tier banks. Thus, the charter covers a small number of selected major relationship banks, split between core banks and second tier banks.

Criteria for the selection of core banks

Our criteria for the selection of our group of core banks were that among all the banks selected, Cookson should have banks with:

(a) An international spread.
(b) The ability to provide the group with substantially all of its on going commercial banking and financing requirements at competitive rates.

These requirements would include, for example, commercial banking and foreign exchange lines, bilateral committed facilities or participation in arranging (e.g. advisory, lead managing, co-managing) private placements, syndicated loans, Eurobond issues, ADRs, credit ratings, commercial paper issues (US or Euro) and other related forms of commercial banking business.

The core banks have been advised that they cannot be guaranteed any business; this must be won on merit which is a function of proven ability and price. Whilst the treasury team continues to ensure that the banks are fully informed of suitable business opportunities, the final selection of a bank for a specific purpose must be, and be seen as, in the best interests of the group. Whilst we will invite our core banks to bid for business (e.g. a commercial banking review or leading a US private placement) we will also invite recognised market leaders in the relevant fields and award the business on merit. Other things being equal, however, we would award the business to a core bank.

It is important for us that the banks positively want to be a member of that select group. We have found that a more lasting relationship develops where a bank makes a positive decision to join, rather than where a bank is a core member by default, that is historically having the level of committed facilities available to the group. Whilst these committed facilities are important, there are many other factors that make for a mutual long term relationship.

Practical implementation of the charter

Once the bank relationship philosophy had been agreed internally, it was relatively straightforward to develop the core bank charter and invite selected banks to be members of the core group. The key driver for ensuring that both the banks and the group's senior executive continue to support the arrangement lies in the way in which the charter is implemented in practice. The best way to describe this is to give examples of how we made it work.

Annual meeting with banks

Each year, after the group's preliminary annual results have been announced, senior representatives of the core and second tier banks are invited to attend, as a group, a presentation on the results by the chairman, group chief executive and group finance director. This meeting enables the banks to listen to an analysis of the results and of the group's strategy and then have the opportunity to raise questions on issues arising from the discussions. This is followed by the group treasurer and the treasury team giving a presentation on treasury strategies and issues.

These meetings enable the banks to meet those other banks within the major relationship banking group and can generate some interesting and lively discussion. We believe that this forum, along with participation by the group's senior executive management, helps reinforce Cookson's commitment to its relationship philosophy. It also gives the banks comfort on meeting their peers, particularly given the quality of the group's bankers.

These meetings have been extremely well received by the banks and we have been actively encouraged to continue with them.

Information update with banks

After the interim results have been announced, the group finance director and group treasurer hold meetings with each core and second tier bank individually. The chief executive also attends, schedule permitting.

The treasury has further meetings throughout the year with each bank; this can be for a general update on matters or if the banks want to discuss something specific. We also keep them fully informed on events within the treasury. Our responsibility is to be 'on call' for our core and second tier banks and, with the banks' account officer, be the key focal points between the two organisations.

We endeavour to ensure that the banks never receive any unpleasant surprises. We are cognisant of the need to comply with Stock Exchange and other regulations but there are times when the banks must hear of events from ourselves, rather than hearing about it elsewhere.

Understanding the Cookson business – site visits

The banks are encouraged to understand our business through site visits. In September 1994 we organised, for our core banks, a two day trip around four of our UK operating sites. The banks told us how beneficial this was from their viewpoint.

These visits also encourage the operating companies. Local managements are justifiably proud of their businesses. To have a group of senior bankers taking an active interest in the business is a motivating factor. It also underscores to the operating companies the role that treasury performs within the group. Although organising such visits can be time consuming, we feel the benefits to both sides fully justify the time expended.

Business opportunities

The banks are kept informed of business opportunities within the group, be it foreign exchange lines for operating companies, banking reviews or financing needs. Our approach in implementing this in practice has been discussed earlier.

Gateway to the group

The treasury acts as 'gateway to the group' for the banks. Where they have specific areas they wish to discuss we will always try to arrange meetings with the appropriate people within the company. Examples could be a tax driven financing scheme or an M&A opportunity. We would ensure that the schemes or proposals would reach, and be responded to by, the right person in the company.

Response time

It is an unwritten rule in treasury that our response to banks, particularly major relationship banks, must be prompt, even if it is a 'no thank you'. As noted earlier, this approach was much appreciated by the banks in 1990 and, indeed, gave the banks confidence that matters at Cookson were, in fact, under control. However, we apply this approach even to more mundane situations.

The practical implementation of the Cookson bank charter will continue to develop over time and in response to what our banks (reasonably) require from us. As noted earlier, first and foremost, we must attend to the best interests of Cookson and its shareholders. The practical application of our philosophy, we believe, meets this key criteria.

Cookson's expectations of core banks

So far the emphasis has been on what Cookson will do for the banks. As in any mutual business relationship, we expect the banks to provide us with a number of services. These include:

(a) Funding at competitive rates.
(b) Providing a range of commercial banking services and products (e.g. trade finance, information on overseas markets, contracts, advisory).

(c) Assisting with the commercial banking arrangements of our operating companies.

(d) Using the banks' expertise on banking structures and systems (domestically or internationally) to enable the operating companies to run more cost effective banking arrangements.

(e) The account officer having sufficient knowledge of the company and sufficient seniority to represent Cookson's interests effectively within the bank.

(f) The account officer, normally based in London, being the person who co-ordinates everything that any branch of that bank is doing with any Cookson company worldwide. This acts as a control mechanism and helps to prevent operating companies from undertaking unauthorised transactions with the banks.

(g) Being in a position to give us prompt responses to our requests or queries, even if it is 'no'.

As with most successful long term relationships, both parties have to work hard in meeting the realistic expectations of each other. Whilst we may both demand and expect a range of services, delivered both promptly and cost effectively, it is incumbent on us to ensure that we keep faith with our bank charter.

Review and change in major relationship banks

Each year we review the performance of our major relationship banks to ensure that both sides continue to benefit from the overall relationship and that both parties wish to continue. Given the close working and open relationship that we adopt throughout the year, this is often a formality. However, we are cognisant of the pressure on banks to satisfy their own shareholders which can translate into the banks shifting their focus of their business or even demanding through their account officer a greater share of our business. It is not in our best interests to have an account officer under pressure, who in turn is trying to put pressure on us. This relationship is bound to fail.

These situations have to be carefully managed and, in order to retain credibility with our other lenders, we have to take a firm line on the practical application of our charter – that our major relationship banks have an opportunity to bid for our commercial banking business but there is never any guarantee that any individual institution will be awarded it.

Over the years, we have had to part company with some of our core and second tier banks. Circumstances leading to this have been different in each case and have involved considerable dialogue with the specific bank, often over a long period of time. Even though the outcome of these discussions is often clear, each situation must be handled with a high degree of sensitivity. The banks with which we deal are major institutions in their own right and they deserve the management time to ensure that the parting is as amicable as possible.

Examples of the circumstances which have led to our changing our core/second tier banks are given below:

(a) The bank's shift away from pure lending.
(b) The bank's inability to make a sufficient total return on its business to justify a large committed funding facility. Our bilateral committed facilities are competitively priced on a stand-alone basis and without any guarantee of future business.
(c) A change in the account officer. This can directly impact the close working relationship between corporate and bank, particularly in the early days of a relationship. The quality of the account officer can also influence the general level of service or response we receive from the banks.
(d) A core bank may want to reduce its committed exposure, given the need to provide competitive pricing on a smaller tranche of funding but retain tangible commitment with the group. This can result in a core bank moving to second tier status.

Under normal circumstances, few banks like being excluded from the company's banking group. Sometimes, however, the situation is inevitable and where this is so, it is best recognised and acted upon quickly.

Benefits of relationship management

We believe that our approach to banking relationship management provides the group with significant benefits. These range from the daily activities performed by our banks including our ability to utilise the banks' knowledge and resources on a wide range of issues (e.g. bank's own domestic banking system; bank presentations at treasury workshops; technical advice; contacts in non-domestic regions). It also makes day-to-day banking relationships pleasant to operate. The real strength of our approach, however, has proved crucial in a number of circumstances:

(a) In the latter part of 1990, our major relationship banks continued support for Cookson and did not make the situation worse for the finance team by hounding them. This relationship, supported by the committed facilities, was crucial to the group at the time.

(b) In November 1994, Cookson and Johnson Matthey were in merger discussions, which were subsequently terminated. However, one option for the merged structure required certain consents from our lending banks as well as the possibility of substantial bridging finance. We spoke with each bank individually and had our consents and offers for bridging finance 'by return'.

(c) In December 1994, we refinanced our committed facilities in order to extend the maturity profile of our debt. We decided to do this by a self-syndication with our major relationship banks. This was completed extremely quickly with similar documentation for each bank.

The value of this 'pay-back' cannot be over-emphasised; it more than justifies the commitment and time of our senior executive and financial management. Whilst we cannot foretell the future, we do know we will continue to need our major relationship banks and therefore will continue with our approach to relationship management.

The banks' perspective

The response from our bankers has been extremely positive and they have regularly re-emphasised their support on our approach to banking relationships. Besides readily obtaining factual information on the company they can actively see our philosophy at work and the commitment that it has from the group's senior management. This proactive management of, and commitment to, banking relationships gives the banks increased confidence in the group. That this is so, has been clearly evidenced from both the tangible support that the banks have given Cookson over the years and their encouragement that we should continue our approach.

Some reflections

The practical application of our banking philosophy works for Cookson; it has the clear endorsement of both our senior executive management and our major relationship banks. It has paid clear dividends in the past; this open dialogue, with a clear statement of what we bring to, and what we expect from, our banking relationships will continue but will evolve as the company develops and the banking market changes.

In the end, we are motivated by doing what we believe is in the best long term interests of the Cookson Group and its shareholders. We believe our approach to banking relationships clearly achieves this overriding criterion. We intend to continue this approach in order to retain the support of the banks, which can never be taken for granted.

The banks clearly endorse our approach; we also believe that it has wider implications in helping enhance Cookson's name in the financial markets for its professional approach and clear strategy on bank relationship management.

10 Ending a relationship

In this chapter we are concerned with the ending of a banking relationship. As Aristotle observed: 'Everything has a beginning, a middle and an end.' While everyone accepts that the relationship may end at some time or another and for one reason or another, seldom, if ever, do the borrower and banker plan for it from the beginning. They would rarely begin a relationship, for instance, by noting down those changes, which should they take place, would cause the reason behind the relationship to be called into question. Rather, they would invariably proceed under the implicit assumption that changes either will not occur or, should they occur, both will be willing and able to adjust in such a way that the relationship will continue to be mutually beneficial.

But Aristotle frequently proves right. Somewhere along the middle of the relationship events take place and changes occur in either the borrower's or banker's situation, none of which were anticipated in the beginning, which profoundly alter the underlying reasons for entering the relationship in the first place. Needs change on the part of the borrower, objectives change on the part of the banker – all of which result in the relationship no longer making sense to either one or the other, or both. The time for ending it is at hand.

As with many a divorce, however, this is not always easy. One party has to take the initiative and is generally the one with the more reasons and the greater incentive for ending the relationship. No matter how it is handled, the other party will often feel aggrieved. And this is frequently compounded by the fact that the party ending the relationship has done relatively better than the other and this, by itself, had contributed to a decline in the usefulness of continuing. Moreover, the party being terminated will generally suffer more than the other, either financially or in terms of prestige.

But change is in the order of things. The better the borrower and the banker understand each other's position and needs, the better they are able to analyse and interpret how these are changing, the better they will both be in anticipating and rationalising the end when it comes. It may not make it any easier, but at least it will not come as a total surprise.

What is a relationship?

Occasional conversation, a lunch now and then do not constitute a banking relationship. The essential ingredient has to be a willingness and ability to do business. This can be in the form of a commitment, either legal or moral, of one party to the other or it can just be an understanding. The form is not as important as the substance.

At one extreme, there may be a relationship but as of yet no business done. At the other, the relationship may have totally ended and yet loans remain outstanding. It is the attitude of the parties towards the future that counts.

The situation may be even more complicated. Both have agreed to do business in one area, but not another; for instance, they are willing to trade currencies but not to lend. Consequently, part of the relationship may be ended, but another part allowed to carry on.

In addition, the relationship may not be ended in a formal sense but nevertheless so changed that it is something entirely new. For instance, when a bank is dropped from the first tier its relationship to the company may change from being on the inside to merely being a part of a syndicate; or in other words, little different from any other market participant.

Reasons for ending relationships

There are a number of reasons why either party may want to end a banking relationship.

From the company's point of view:

(a) The company may have outgrown the resources of the bank.
(b) The company's banking relationships may have become so extensive and complicated that they need to be rationalised.
(c) The bank may have repeatedly shown that it cannot perform its tasks efficiently.
(d) The bank may have disbanded or downgraded products or services that the corporation views as essential.
(e) The bank's situation may have so deteriorated that it can no longer be relied upon to honour its commitments.

(f) The bank may have an inherent conflict of interest which obviates a normal relationship.

From the bank's point of view:

(a) The credit standing of the company may have materially changed for the worse.
(b) The bank may have changed its strategic orientation and no longer want to serve the industry or the company.
(c) The bank may no longer have the resources to make it a meaningful relationship.
(d) The account may have proven unprofitable, with little prospect of improving.
(e) The integrity of the company's officers may have been called into question.

Failure to establish a strong relationship

Anyone who has ever glanced at a league table of the world's banks knows that there is no shortage of potential bank lenders. Not so long ago, within the memory of some senior financial executives, it was the borrower who warmed a cold marble bench in the anteroom of the banker's office, mentally rehearsing the case for more funds. Then competitive pressures changed all that – at least for the credit worthy corporation. Companies were overwhelmed with offers of finance to the point where the term 'relationship banking' became meaningless. Now, the term is back in favour but many bankers are sceptical.

But does either party really know what they are getting into? Does the company understand what the bank expects to make from this relationship? Does it understand how this will take place, what is required of it? Does the bank fully understand the dynamics of the company and its industry – what might be required during a downturn, what risks and exposure might have to be assumed?

Some banking relationships are, of course, flawed from the start. It is a cause of a relationship entered into on the basis of unrealistic expectations or simple wishful thinking. When there never is a proper, realistic beginning, with both parties overtly committing themselves to specific areas of interest, knowing each other's strengths and weaknesses, the end can be all but preordained. Disillusionment can quickly set in and divorce becomes only a matter of time.

Competitive pressures have led many banks to establish a semblance of expertise in most mainstream areas of banking. Many have branches worldwide and lay claim to a global reach. Account officers are told that they can claim their bank offers practically every product and service, almost everywhere in the world, that the company would need or want. But setting up a department is not necessarily acquiring expertise; having branches is not necessarily being truly global.

But it is not all the bank's fault. Some of the blame rests with the treasurer who has failed to independently assess the strengths and weaknesses of the bank, to know the bank as well as it tries to know the company. There are those treasurers who merely hold court for their bankers when they call, feeding their ego rather than their store of knowledge. They either have the luxury of nothing very important to do or run the risk of being rudely disappointed by the unexpected results they get.

The divergence between expectations and reality is frequently the cause for ending a relationship. The excuse may be one of the reasons we listed earlier in this chapter, but the real cause is quite different. It is a case of an ending without a proper beginning.

Reduction and restructuring of banking relationships

More and more treasurers are beginning to operate a tiered system with their banks. This is where key relationship banks are chosen to be much closer to the group than others. One of the important benefits of this approach is in terms of time management; as a practical matter a treasurer can only deal effectively with a limited number of banks.

In return for their privileged position, key relationship banks will be expected to offer more relevant, tailor-made products, based on the particular requirements of the Group: preferential allocation of limited resources such as export finance for 'difficult' countries or loans if there is a credit squeeze; consistent competitive pricing; standard documentation; and direct dealing lines. In return the bank will expect an opportunity to quote in most areas where it is competent, and that the group will not use other banks just to secure minor cost savings.

For many large companies there will have to be a hard pruning of existing relationships. Marginal accounts will have to be either terminated or put into a second class status. Account officers will have to be told to call less frequently and to talk with less senior people. They will have to be informed that they can expect fewer chances to bid for certain types of business.

In many cases, this will just formalise what has already happened *de facto*. The selection of the key banks will normally be based on the past usefulness of existing relationships. Deselected banks will probably not be too surprised, but that will not ease their pain of losing apparent status, which is only natural.

The sophisticated corporation will of course handle these rearrangements with the utmost tact and discretion. It will be as open as possible about the selection process, the criteria used and what could possibly in the future call for a revision of the list. The alert bank will not take its rejection as an affront, but will gracefully accept its position and possibly work up a plan to eventually reverse it. Both parties will recognise the importance of maintaining a low level contact, just to preserve their options for the future. Handled correctly, such a reordering of banking relationships should not be a traumatic event, but rather viewed for what it is: a rational, pragmatic and necessary restructuring.

A change of direction

Nor will such a change be only instigated by the company. It will have escaped no treasurer that the banking community is undergoing some fundamental changes. Some of these are self-induced by the banks and some are the product of basic changes in how corporations source their funds.

Most commercial banks have concluded that they can no longer offer every service to every potential customer. To be cost effective, they, like others, have to concentrate their efforts by offering selected services targeted to selected customers. This often requires a new strategic orientation and a new organisational structure. It would be a happy coincidence if all existing banking relationships fitted well into the new direction of the bank.

Terminating or modifying relationships under these circumstances should not be too difficult or endanger the bank's existing customers. Most will be able to find alternative banking sources given a decent lead time and a good introduction. Sometimes too, the relationship has reached a natural end for both parties and a formal recognition of this can be quite friendly since both sides recognise they may meet again in different circumstances.

Sometimes, however, this is not the way it is handled. The bank is so caught up in its internal problems, so self-centred, that notification is by way of a curt letter demanding immediate repayment. The account officer, if he or she still exists within the organisation, does not care. The bank acts as if there is no tomorrow; what terminated customers say to others does not count.

It is assumed that that a once valued customer will never be valued again. It is a short term policy followed by bank officers with short term career prospects. Only the long term shareholders of the bank will suffer.

Finally, some banks spend more time explaining their new rocket age reorganisation (and reorganisations occur in the order of once every two years or so) than in discussing real business. With reorganisation comes new faces. Account officers change with the rapidity of a revolving door. One just gets up to speed with the corporation's business before he or she is reorganised away. Banks, who rely on frequent changes to mask deep seated deficiencies, should not be surprised when their favoured targets turn the tables and instead target them – for deselection.

A change of personalities

As every banker and treasurer knows, a banking relationship often boils down to the personalities involved. Interpersonal skills are often a deciding factor in whether there is a beneficial relationship or nothing at all. The nature of the dealings are such that the key individuals involved can heavily influence the nature of the relationship. Changing personnel on either side can affect a relationship, for better or worse.

In establishing and maintaining relationships a treasurer should, to the extent possible, be open about likely areas of business, and the prospects for business. This will allow the banker to concentrate his efforts and avoid blind alleys. Likewise, the banker should be honest about the bank's capabilities. He/she should not accept business the bank cannot handle well.

Over time, following this sensible approach, a rapport will be built up between banker and treasurer. A mutual respect and confidence will be established, where one can level with the other, without it being misconstrued and damaging the overall relationship. Not that the treasurer ever reveals all or that the banker never says no, but both will find that balance between being too demanding and not demanding enough. Neither, of course, wants the other to tell his chairman that he is just marvellous or that he is just impossible to work with. The first implies giving away too much; the second, arrogance.

For it to work, both treasurer and banker have to view it as a long term relationship. Both must realise that it will not work if either is opportunistic or less than above board in his or her dealing. Both have to adopt the objective of guarding their personal reputation as well as that of their institution, taking into account that memories can be long and the financial and corporate community surprisingly small and close-knit when it comes to ethical dealing.

The relationship between the company and the bank is of course many layered. Each chairman will play a part, as will senior directors and other colleagues. Being aware of the role each should play or want to play is crucial to the relationship. Both banker and treasurer must keep this in mind as well as the practical limits of each of their own authority and responsibility. It will weaken the position of either to be shown to be either constantly overstepping his/her authority or continually indecisive on matters clearly within his/her area of responsibility.

Not everyone is endowed with the skills to do this well. When a relatively less skilled person replaces a skilled one, there is liable to be a deterioration in the relationship. Most of the time, the individuals adjust and simply accept the situation. But some of the time, it is necessary or better to ask for another change. Handled tactfully, this should not be a calamitous event, but viewed as the best course for maintaining the relationship. Sometimes requisite skill is simply not enough. Everyone knows that some personalities just don't mix, no matter how skilled each may be. It will take a very keen observer of human nature to detect what is really going on in many of these cases.

Rarely will either the treasurer or banker want to admit that they simply do not like one another. Rather, they will more often put it down to the 'glaring incompetence' of the other party, building a case to support their position out of little incidents where the other party has purportedly failed to perform satisfactorily.

These situations often snowball, growing worse and worse, until a total rupture is threatened, unless one of the parties is removed. Rightly or wrongly, it is generally the banker that has to give way, no matter who may be more at fault. The banker's superiors should recognise the situation for what it is – a personality clash – no more avoidable in life than taxes.

Misinformation

In most banking relationships and negotiations, the company will have to present its plans to its bankers. This will include financial forecasts and critical elements of the business plan. While there is generally no reason to divulge company secrets, particularly not to an international syndicate of banks, enough will have to be said to make the corporation bankable.

This is an ongoing process. A formal presentation will probably be made at least annually and may be done by the finance director or even the chairman. In between presentations, the treasurer will update the banker during a meeting or over lunch on how things are going.

Most of these sessions are routine, relaxed affairs, viewed by bankers as part of their due diligence responsibility. It is only when the company encounters a major problem that the importance and intensity of these meetings take on a different meaning. The company spends days and weeks preparing itself, and the presentation is massaged by all the key officers, for a lot may be at stake.

The bank probably fields more staff than just the account officer to hear what the company has to say. The files are reviewed with care and pertinent questions are prepared and circulated within the bank. The bank reviews its options and prepares itself for a major decision after the meeting regarding the future of the relationship.

What the company finally decides to present is not as clear cut as simply picking the truth. Forecasts are based on assumptions, some of which may be within the control of the company, but many of which are not. Usually the chairman and president will have an upbeat scenario (they would not have their jobs if they did not). The finance director, on the other hand, will see all the downside risks (and this is his/her job as well). The 'truth' may unfold along one line or the other or entirely differently.

Seldom will the chairman allow the finance director to present a horror story. In the first place, the chairman does not truly believe it and in the second, he fears it will scare off the banks. And this 'gut' view that banks will discount whatever they are told is probably right. Better to discount a mildly optimistic forecast than a mildly pessimistic one.

The finance director will resist, however, giving the upbeat view of the chairman. The finance director would rather be in the position of explaining positive variances to the banker during subsequent meetings rather than negative ones. What the finance director can negotiate out of the chairman will depend on his or her stature within the group and the confidence the chairman has in his/her judgement and skill in assessing and handling the banks.

It is important to realise that this is not necessarily a question of testing or pitting one person's honesty or integrity against another. Both may truly believe that their forecast will be close to the mark.

Certainly, there is a downside to every forecast, but there may be an upside as well. The future is forever uncertain.

But both will hopefully remember that bankers have large filing cabinets. They keep what they are given; they note what they are told. They will require continual updating and cogent explanations for any deviations from plan. Too many deviations and our chairman or finance director risks being branded as either a liar or a fool, but in either event, not someone to do business with. Bankers are apt to accept one or two really bad forecasts, but after that, they will probably want to end the relationship.

Poor performance

Dropping a bank because of poor performance is generally not something that happens overnight. It is more often than not the accumulation of a number of small errors or incidents, which are repeated over a number of months or years and which are seemingly uncorrectable by the bank's management. Back office mistakes are the most irritating of all since they all seem so trivial, but as we saw in Chapter 2 changing the bank at the centre of the company's payment systems is not easy.

The problem is brought to the attention of the bank's account officer. He or she tries to fix it internally, telling the client that it is now all in order, only to hear some weeks later that the problem has recurred. The process goes on and on until finally the client gives up the unequal struggle.

The client may not entirely cut the relationship at this point, however, fearing that the bank may again insist on continuing its hopeless quest to sort itself out. Rather, it may be more cunning, wait a while and then pick another issue, over which the bank has little or nothing to say, as the one for severing the relationship; for instance, that it is under orders to consolidate its banking relations. The client gets what it wants, but avoids an unpleasant confrontation.

Sometimes, of course, the client may be more forthright and make its reasons for leaving quite explicit, if for no other reason than the desire to vent its frustration. Whether this will have any salutary effect on the bank, however, is questionable. What it was unable to correct before, after repeated efforts, probably remains uncorrectable now. Only a concentrated management effort will work. As they ignored all the warning signs before, it is unlikely they will take notice now.

Poor profitability

Everyone enjoys something for nothing whether it be free advice, free services or free lines of credit. Sometimes banks will begin relationships offering all three. But this cannot go on for ever. At some point, the bank has to begin making a respectable return or it will not be able to cover its overheads.

Of course, it is not up to the corporation to make sure the bank is being adequately compensated. It is in the corporation's interest to get the cheapest services and loans and it will negotiate with its bankers, playing one off against another, to do just that. Moreover, history has shown that past generosity does not necessarily buy undying future loyalty.

But no relationship will last if one of the parties gets little out of it. While it can be argued that ideally every deal should stand by itself, this is seldom possible. Certain services are expected from a banking relationship which are impossible to invoice separately. So the banks naturally turn to the overall profitability of the account.

It is, of course, not easy to measure account profitability and different banks will approach it in different ways. Banks have recently devoted massive resources on accounts measurement systems. Whether a foreign exchange transaction makes or loses money will depend on the skill of the bank's dealers. There is no way a company can know the bank's profitability on currency deals. But having volume does make it possible to make money and this is often what the account officer looks at.

Most banks do not insist on directed business. Most expect to compete for the business that the corporation has to offer. What they are really looking for in the final analysis is the opportunity to compete. Likewise, most banks do not look for the company to pay spreads in excess of the market. They expect to compete here as well. But what they will not tolerate is for the company to habitually award its business to just the lowest bidder without taking into account the rest of the relationship.

It is not an easy balance for the company to make. What are these other services worth? Seldom do corporations keep journals or logs of all the contacts between them and their bankers and try to price out the value of these contacts. Bankers are always saying they want more of the business, more opportunities to quote and more chances to look at deals. It is difficult for the treasurer to judge if he or she is showing them enough, in view of the overall relationship, or not enough. Since they all make the same demand, not everyone can be satisfied all of the time.

The one thing most companies do, however, is respect the bank that brings them an unusual deal. Most are prepared to compensate the bank for initiative, within reason; few will take the idea and shop it around for a better price, although bankers often suspect them of doing so, and the alert treasurer is generally quick to point out to the banker if the proposal being made is not really a proprietary product, but already well promoted in the market by others. Occasionally this will lead to a misunderstanding, but the relationship is usually strong enough to withstand minor shocks.

But the time does come when a bank, generally after many meetings and warnings, decides that it is a hopelessly losing proposition to continue nursing a sick account. The effort expended is simply not compensated by the business received. It is not a decision taken lightly, for the bank is aware of the time spent in trying to develop the account. It knows that breaking the relationship will be more or less lasting, that restoring broken relationships is often impossible before the personalities involved are either gone or retired. But since there is no point in running a continual loss leader and since correcting the situation has been tried and failed, there is little other alternative open to the bank. Something for nothing is not for ever.

Conflicts of interest

The Chinese made very curious walls. They were meant to separate and isolate, but without being noticed. Banks insist walls exist within their organisations, but many companies remain sceptical of their efficiency. It runs counter to corporate philosophy to have part of the company isolated from the rest, hence their scepticism.

The idea is that the company can tell all to the bank's account officer, but none of this will filter through to the bank's corporate finance staff, who might be working down the hall with a potential raider in preparing a hostile bid to take over the corporation. It may be true that the two staffs do not talk to one another, but it is hard for a corporation to believe that the bank is not using all its available resources and information in deciding whether to take the risk of financing the raider's bid.

On the announcement of a hostile bid, it would be a very magnanimous management that did not immediately sever its relationship with the bank. And it would be very unsuspecting management that told all to a bank known to be active in financing hostile takeovers.

The fact that a bank becomes active in pursuing hostile bids has to cause concern on the part of companies vulnerable to them. While this concern will probably not lead to a rupture of relations, it will dampen the dialogue and lessen the interdependency between the two. The bank's support will come to mean less to the corporation and the account's profitability will suffer. The relationship may eventually end on this note rather than on the original reason.

This is the most severe form of conflict of interest but another more common concern for companies is to prevent the seepage of confidential information about an equity matter to the 'market' side in a bank. This problem has been greatly increased in the 1990s because of the development of universal banking whereby commercial, investment and funds management functions are all part of the same bank.

An inherently unstable system

Scientists describe a system as 'stable' when it has a tendency to return to equilibrium after a disturbance and 'unstable' when it has a tendency to run away to the extremes. Under this definition, bank relations can be described as inherently unstable.

When things are going well, there is no shortage of banks willing and eager to loan. Lending margins decrease as one bank competes with another for the business. The corporation, already doing well, also enjoys a surfeit of cheap funds.

On the other hand, when difficulties are encountered, not only will the banks want to raise their margins, some will also want to cancel their lines. As one bank departs, others begin to wonder if it is worth staying; some of them are likely to want to leave as well. Pretty soon, if not checked, there will be a stampede of bankers to the door. The company's earnings problem is first compounded by higher interest rates and then it is liable to turn into a full blown liquidity, survival problem.

It is easy enough to criticise the banks for creating the crises. However, put in perspective, it must be remembered that, for the most part, banks lend at margins that are not anywhere near high enough to compensate for the loss of principal. They make their initial lending judgements based on a reasonable assurance of the safety of principal, so when that is threatened, their reaction is often one of 'cut and run'.

The problem is that not every bank can successfully follow this course at the same time. What is more, they all know it. So there is a temptation to use any amount of subterfuge to sneak out quickly and quietly while the corporation and the other bankers are looking the other way.

Never say never

The situation has been studied, the options reviewed and now the decision made. The time is at hand to end the relationship. The only question remaining is how to handle it.

No one likes rejection, but there is no getting around the fact that one party is going to have to reject the other. Should the relationship have so deteriorated that both parties are reconciled to parting, and therefore it is just a question of which one will take the initiative, then there will be little reason for drama or recriminations.

But this is often not the case. One party is frequently at a disadvantage and more vulnerable than the other – at least for the time being. What is important for the initiator to consider is whether and by what means the relationship can be best terminated without causing permanent hard feelings, for there may come a day when it is in its interest to try and restore it. This calls for consideration, tact and sensitivity. A forthright, clear statement of the reasons followed by an expression of regret works best.

It does not always work this way, however. Sometimes, the initiator acts as if there is no tomorrow. No cogent reason is offered; no explanation beyond the banal. Handled in this way, the whole affair is not so much a simple, businesslike suspension of the relationship as an abrupt rupture.

Treasurers who have been through the credit cycle become quite cynical about the process. At first, the bank eagerly solicits the business, but when things get tough, the bank cuts the line overnight. Then, when things get back to normal, the bank walks in as if nothing has happened soliciting the business again. Given the turnover at the bank, however, it is never the same face all three times. That makes it easy for the new person to disown the actions of the old – 'it will never happen again, we've changed our policy and personnel, believe me.'

Banks pick up reputations for solidity and loyalty. Their tactics for ending relationships become known. Treasurers of troubled companies are well advised not to begin a relationship with a recognised short termer. It will only end in tears.

Banks face a different, but similar problem. Is it really worth getting involved with a cut throat corporation that is out to skin the bank on every deal? Do leopards change their spots or will your relationship turn out like all the others – on the scrap heap after a lot of wasted time and effort? Perhaps it is better not to begin.

The best time for considering how a relationship might end is at the beginning. One can then be dispassionate, consider the likelihood of an early or awkward end and make a rational decision. But this is easier said than done. Businesspeople and bankers are optimists by nature and optimists do not like dwelling on the dark side. Unlike Aristotle, they only like seeing the beginning and the middle. They hope against hope that there will be no end.

11 Looking ahead

Now it is time to look ahead. Banking is a cyclical business. Since the recession of 1990/91 when liquidity was tight and margins reasonable, banks have seen their margins decline to such an extent that they cannot make money on loans to large corporations. They have therefore been forced to seek money making opportunities in other areas such as the capital markets and insurance whilst still nursing relationships with their large corporate clients. At some point, as we have seen in the past, there will be a deal too far and suddenly liquidity will tighten and margins will move out again. Such is the nature of commercial banking. It is the inevitable consequence of having too many banks. As these economic cycles have continued, however, there has been a longer cycle of change in the banking industry brought about by both competition and regulation. In this chapter we explore these changes and the possible effects they will have on banking relationships.

Will fewer and bigger banks affect banking relationships?

We have already seen substantial mergers taking place over the last two to three years. In the United States where there is plenty of scope for bank mergers – there are still nearly 10 000 federally insured commercial banks – there has been dramatic activity at the big bank level, culminating in the recent merger of Chemical and Chase Manhattan. Various Japanese banks have merged, some for strategic reasons but others because of loan losses; and in the UK we have seen the loss of independence of some of the biggest merchant banking names and the merger of Lloyds and TSB. This activity looks set to continue because by their very nature mergers tend to unsettle other banks, which previously looked on those that have merged as equals. Yet none of these mergers of commercial banks are transnational which is how real savings could be made, especially within Europe. Such mergers appear too difficult to implement. Instead, banks are buying investment banks, insurance companies and building societies to build financial conglomerates.

How is this activity likely to affect banking relationships? The concept of one-stop banking is, as we have seen earlier, not always popular on the corporate side. Large companies like to deal with a number of financial institutions if only to keep their options open. On the investment banking level too the relationship between the individuals is often all-important so that mergers of banking institutions are likely to see the movement of teams of players from one institution to another. Indeed, in London and New York this has been going on for the last 10 to 20 years. It is interesting that Deutsche Bank which had largely always grown its own talent has set out to join the giants of global universal banking, by reportedly being prepared to spend up to £500 million on recruiting key players from other banks. This activity therefore may well put a strain on banking relationships. As the merger process continues obviously the amount of competition between banks will reduce, but there is a long way to go before this will reach the stage where it seriously increases costs to the large corporate sector.

Corporates might well ask too whether this is not a replay of what happened in their sector in the 1980s when mergers and acquisitions produced ever larger companies. The 1990s have seen a reversal of this trend as companies both in the US and the UK have demerged to increase effectiveness and shareholder value – an important factor in Anglo-Saxon corporate thinking. In the corporate world, big is no longer necessarily beautiful. Thus it is hardly revolutionary to suggest that the turn of the century may indeed see the first bank demergers as boards begin to realise how difficult it is to lead banks with quite disparate skill requirements ranging from trading to selling products, from offering a service to corporates to retail banking.

Another aspect of the present wave of activity is that the retail sector is being driven more and more into specialised functions underpinned by technology. This is a worldwide phenomenon. More and more players are entering the personal finance sector and not all of them well known financial institutions; for example in the UK, Marks & Spencer has already established a strong presence in the financial retail sector and if present trends continue it cannot be long before it and other retailers are developing retail banking services to rival those of the traditional banks. J Sainsbury, another leading UK retailing group, announced its intention to launch a fully licensed retail bank early in 1997. Yet further competition is on the horizon as the potential for Internet banking is realised. Over 150 European banks have sites on the Internet, with many preparing to spend significant sums to be a real player.

Every commercial bank expects there to be further substantial job losses, especially in the retail sector as technology allows the customer to access accounts without using a bank. Remaining staff in the retail sector will increasingly be salespeople. The effect of this may be that the previously large pool of talent with broad banking skills, which was available for the wholesale side of the bank, will dry up.

The big banks are therefore beset with two difficulties: increased competition at the retail end which for years was a sleepy and reactive sector; and the need to build the capital base even further to be able to compete for large corporate clients on a global basis. Here is perhaps the most obvious potential point of demerger for the future – between the retail and wholesale arms.

Whilst banks continue to pay close attention to the wishes of their big corporate clients, they have come to recognise that decent profits are more likely to come from transactions rather than lending. Corporate bankers are therefore increasingly looking to the mid-corporate market for real lending returns. This market – the *Mittelstand* in Germany – has long been seen as a crucial contributor to a successful economy. In the USA this market has been taken care of by local and regional banks. In the UK such companies were dealt with at branch level – increasingly the poor relation of global 'big city' banking; now they enjoy attention at the most senior levels of banks. The reason is simple: the banking is profitable and the clients increasingly sophisticated. Cash management systems, foreign exchange and trade services, and working capital management are areas where the banks can add value to smaller companies' operations. Banks are also offering choice. The client can choose levels of service and pay accordingly. For the banks this business is very profitable and is worth investment in both people and systems.

A new breed of relationship manager has emerged based on regional offices with more sophisticated services. These have largely taken the place of old-type bank managers who knew the owner and handled his/her personal financial affairs. The relationship manager will typically handle a range of clients, some big and some quite small (£1 million plus), and is in a good position to pass on 'best practice' from more sophisticated to less sophisticated companies. This 'management' education theme makes good sense from the banks' viewpoint since it enables them to alert companies to danger signals arising from poor debtor management or weak cash flows.

This trend is another indication of the segmentation that is taking place in big banks.

The road ahead for the banking industry is therefore full of challenges. Old hands would argue, 'when was it ever not?' George Rae writing in 1885 in *The Country Banker* perhaps said it all:

> Let your device as a banker be that of the strong man armed, and your motto AYE READY. You will not otherwise be prepared, at all points and all times, to encounter and overcome the difficulties which may be in store for banking in the large uncertainties of the future. Above all things, in the regulation of your finances, place no reliance on the chapter of accidents for seeing you through.

Regulation and the level playing field

As we saw in Chapter 4, the introduction of the BIS rules on capital adequacy soon influenced the way in which banks treated corporate debt. These rules have now been incorporated into the European Union's Capital Adequacy Directive and the expectation is that the BIS rules will eventually produce a level playing field between all banking competitors. Progress has therefore been made in this direction but not yet by all the central banks involved. The Japanese in particular have been reluctant to give a full picture and it is only in the last few months that, for example, the full extent of Japanese bank loan losses in property enterprises has been brought out into the open. Banks are also being driven towards adopting normal accounting standards where the Anglo/US accounting regime is in the driving seat. This means an attack on secret provisions which allowed the banks to smooth out their results. Formerly, these were encouraged by central banks because it avoided sharp downturns or losses which might have affected confidence in the banking system. Nowadays with the level of regulation in banks at an ever increasing intensity most banking authorities are encouraging the concept of a true and fair view and a future without secret provisions.

So whilst trends are in the right direction it will be some years before we reach the stage where banking worldwide is playing on a level field. Whilst most companies would welcome this trend it is likely to bring them one disadvantage. It will be increasingly difficult for banks to play the 'loss leader' role which would seem to lead to some decline in the level of competition.

European monetary union

Enterprises as large as the proposed European monetary union have to be driven by political willpower. Given the disadvantages and risks involved no commercial enterprise would be able to agree in timely fashion to a deal which suited all the parties. At the moment the political willpower to set up the monetary union is clearly present in Germany and France and some other members of the European Union but not in others, notably the UK. In 1997 there appears to be an almost unstoppable will to go ahead in 1999. The financial and technical problems involved are awesome. For example, although monetary union is scheduled to start in 1999 the new currency will not be available until the year 2002. This is because it will take all this time for the required amount of currency to be minted. Furthermore, all the banking systems regarding transfers etc will require years of development and enormous sums of money. The UK alone is likely to spend billions of pounds equipping itself for monetary union, even assuming it is not a member. Indeed, it is not difficult to make the case that those members of the EU that will not be joining monetary union will have a double problem and incur even greater expense. Furthermore, the first signs are appearing of the penalties that countries outside EMU will face. The new payments system – Target – was assumed to be open to all EU members. This is now in doubt, however, as 'insiders' demand restricted access for 'outsiders'. The implications of this are considerable.

It is not hard to imagine therefore that with the banking industry grappling with the problems of equipping itself for monetary union in a very short timescale, the effect on the corporate side is likely to be significant. Nor is it likely that companies will be able to gear themselves up very quickly since they will want to know quite how the banking industry is going to set out its stall; indeed more fundamentally whether their home base is 'in' or 'out'. In short, the effect on the corporate side of monetary union is that much attention and resource will have to be devoted to this topic over at least a five year period.

Whither banking relationships?

In the midst of all this change is there a place for old-fashioned banking relationships? The short answer is yes; indeed they are going to grow in importance. It has been a thrust of this book that despite the swings and roundabouts in relationships brought about by cycles, recessions and changes in margins, the successful company has been one that has always been able to rely on liquidity and the support of its banks. Writer after writer has stressed the importance of being open with information – the 'no surprises' policy. This is two sided. Good banking relationships imply trust and trust develops when two people like and respect each other. Talk to senior bankers and it becomes immediately apparent how important it is for them that they know the senior people in a company – the treasurer, the finance director and the chief executive. They also want to understand the business and the inherent risks in that business so that they can relate them to the risks in their own business.

John Melbourn, immediate Past President of the Chartered Institute of Bankers and until recently, Deputy Group Chief Executive of NatWest, summed up his views as follows:

> My own view is that if one holds oneself out to be a 'rainy day' banker, then that imposes a degree of discipline over and above the norm; to be able to fulfil such an ambition one can only do so by exhibiting, on a constant basis, a degree of personal and corporate professionalism which is above the median. The essential ingredient is to be readily available at all times, even at times of great inconvenience. The last thing a client wants to hear if he has a particular need or is in trouble, is that the banker is rather busy and can see him next Friday week! What he wants is a sympathetic and immediate hearing; he wants considered, professional advice and help of an objective nature; sometimes that advice relays unpalatable facts.

Modern banking puts greater emphasis on risk management. Some of this is highly technical and very bound up in numbers, but this only forms the basis of the assessment. More important is the assessment of quality of integrity and knowledge of the business. The senior management of the company needs to be able to rely on the absolute integrity of its bankers. The company will also keep an eye on credit ratings and will want to be assured that the bank is in this relationship for the long term. The worst thing for the company is to spend a lot of time on developing relationships with a bank which then suddenly changes direction and moves away for strategic reasons. The company will look to the bank as part of its financial strategy. In good times it will be offering services and advice that the company will find valuable. In bad times the bank will give its support willingly. It is important therefore that the company seeks its banks carefully. It should also ensure that its lead bank is highly respected so that other banks all want to follow its lead.

When rapid changes are happening in the banking industry, banking relationships are even more important because they provide a stable basis on which financial decisions can be taken.

Index

Printed and bound by CPI Group (UK) Ltd, Croydon, CR0 4YY

11/05/2025

01866608-0001